AF432303

Low Carb Instant Pot Cookbook

100 Quick and Easy Low Carb Recipes to Lose Weight and Heal Your Body

Lindsey Page

Table of Contents

CHAPTER FIVE

x

CHAPTER ONE

An Overview of the Low Carb Diet

A low carb diet will restrict the amount of carbohydrates you eat, asking you to focus instead on lean proteins, healthy fats and high fiber vegetables that have little sugar. There are dozens of varieties of low carb diets on the market. Some of them will give you a specific number of carbohydrates that you are not to exceed and others will have a strict list of foods you absolutely may not eat. Remember that a low carb diet is not the same as a no carb diet. You still want to get a few complex carbohydrates into your system in the forms of leafy green veggies and fruits like berries and melon. It's best to simply be mindful of the carbs you are eating and to choose different food groups when planning meals and snacks.

Why Follow a Low Carb Diet?

Most people choose to adopt a low carb eating plan when they want to lose weight. If you have diabetes or your doctor has diagnosed you as pre-diabetic, a low carb diet may be prescribed. That's because this type of eating plan will reduce the levels of glucose that's held in your blood. Insulin levels will drop when you reduce the amount of carbohydrates you eat. People who are overweight also benefit from low carb diets because their blood pressure goes down. High blood pressure is one of the leading causes of strokes and it also contributes to heart disease. The change in your metabolism when you focus on low carb eating can help bring down your blood pressure and allow your heart to function better. This is especially true for people struggling with obesity.

Low Carb Eating: Foods to Enjoy

Proteins and fats are the focus when you're enjoying a low carb lifestyle. You can fill up on all the meats you like, whether that's ground beef, steak, pork chops, chicken, turkey, veal, or bison. If you've never tried a bison burger before, now might be a good time. Ostrich patties are also high in protein and full of flavor. Fish is another source of protein. You can eat all your favorite seafoods, including shrimp and lobster, crab and tilapia or salmon and swordfish. Eggs are also an excellent source of both protein and fat, so incorporate those into your meals and snacks whenever possible. All of this protein will leave you feeling full and satisfied, which will help you avoid the junk food that you don't want to eat.

Vegetables that are low in starch are also encouraged on a low carb diet. These include spinach, broccoli, kale, artichokes, asparagus, mushrooms, onions, celery, and tomato. According to the American Diabetes Association, these vegetables are low in carbohydrates and sugar but high in vitamins, fiber, and phytochemicals.

Fruits can be tricky when you're following a low carb diet because they are packed with natural sugars and high in carbohydrates. Decide whether you're going to avoid fruit altogether or allow yourself a little. The fruits lowest in carbs are blueberries, raspberries, and cantaloupe.

Low Carb Eating: Foods to Avoid

When you're eating low carb, prepare to say goodbye to breads, grains, milk and legumes. No pasta, no potatoes, and no rice. Even apples and bananas, which are often celebrated on weight loss diets, are to be avoided because of their sugar and carb content. These are foods you will want to avoid, or at least limit. The things you want to avoid completely are the foods that come prepackaged or processed. Cookies, chips, crackers, and even cans of soup or tomato sauce are often loaded with additional simple carbohydrates that you don't need.

CHAPTER TWO

Introduction to the Instant Pot

The Instant Pot is a programmable electric pressure cooker that can be used as a slow cooker, rice cooker, and steamer. It is also designed to make yogurt, sauté and brown vegetables and meats, and keep meals warm.

Benefits of Using Instant Pot

Cook faster

If you're not familiar with the mechanics of a pressure cooker, they're pretty simple. The food is cooked inside a pot at high heat, and the steam that builds up inside that sealed environment conducts all the cooking. Because the Instant Pot is a sealed container, the temperature of the liquids in the pot can exceed that of boiling water. Because the food is in a hotter environment, it cooks faster.

Easy to use

The menu interface on the front of the Instant Pot has settings that are similar to a microwave oven, and is very easy to use. If a recipe calls for searing meat first and then slow cooking it afterwards, you can do this easily with the pot. Instant Pot makes it possible for home cooks to create complex meals in just one pot. For many of us, this also means not having to wash too many pots after dinner. In addition, cleaning the pot is a breeze and you won't need to exert too much effort when scrubbing it down.

An Instant Pot can save kitchen space as you no longer need to have multiple appliances. This means you don't need to have a separate rice cooker, slow cooker, or yogurt maker. The pot does all these things for you. If you're single and you don't do a lot of cooking, this is also a great way to avoid spending lots of money on appliances that you seldom use.

How to Use an Instant Pot

Instant Pot buttons

There are manual settings, as well as a full range of pre-selected cooking routines that you can program with the push of a single button. A timer can even delay the start time for up to 24 hours. Below are the standard buttons that make using the Instant Pot such a pleasure:

MANUAL: this button is used when you want to adjust the pressure and cooking time. The majority of recipes in this book use the Manual setting.

SAUTÉ: this function sautés and can be adjusted up to **browning** or down to **simmer.** The button is also used to reheat food and to thicken sauces.

SLOW COOK: this button turns the Instant Pot into a slow cooker. When using this setting, you must turn the pressure release handle to the Venting position.

KEEP WARM/CANCEL: this button cancels a prior function or keeps the food warm.

SOUP: this function prepares soups at high pressure for 30 minutes. The time can be manually adjusted by using the "-" or "+" buttons.

MEAT/STEW: this button cooks meats at high pressure for 35 minutes. Cooking time can be adjusted manually.

BEAN/CHILI: this button prepares beans at high pressure for 30 minutes. Cooking time can be adjusted manually.

POULTRY: this button cooks chicken at high pressure for 15 minutes. Cooking time can be adjusted manually.

RICE: this function prepares white rice; the cooking time cannot be adjusted manually.

MULTIGRAIN: this function cooks at high pressure for 40 minutes. Cooking time can be adjusted manually.

PORRIDGE: this function cooks porridge at high pressure for 20 minutes. Cooking time can be adjusted manually.

STEAM: this button is used to steam foods such as vegetables in a steamer basket. It cooks at high pressure for 10 minutes.

Pressure release methods

There are two ways to release pressure in an Instant Pot: the "quick pressure release" or the "natural pressure release." The "quick pressure release" happens when the pressure valve is opened manually, and the steam is released quickly. As the steam is released, so is the pressure. When all of the pressure is released, the float valve sinks and the lid is unlocked. For safety's sake, there is no way for the lid to open until the float valve drops. Some steam will be given off, so don't stick your face too close just yet.

The "natural pressure release" happens when you let the pressure decrease without opening the pressure valve. After the allotted cooking time, the Instant Pot automatically switches from cooking mode to the "Keep Warm" mode. During this time, the pressure naturally drops. How long this takes depends on how much liquid is in the pot. It can take anywhere from ten minutes to half an hour. The float valve will drop when it is time.

What specific release method should you use? For vegetables, it is best to use the "quick pressure release," since vegetables will get soggy if overcooked. The "natural pressure release" method is a great way to let meats, soups, and stews simmer.

Tips for Cooking in Instant Pot

While it does many things with ease, the Instant Pot is especially well-suited towards the creation of soups, chilis, and stews made from scratch. Its ability to soften up unsoaked beans, while all the other ingredients cook, is a real bonus for busy people. It can also turn even the toughest cut of meat into fall-off-the-bone perfection in very short order, which makes it ideal for things such as spare ribs. However, certain cuts of meat such as tender steaks are better cooked on a grill. Pasta is also easier to cook using the standard boiling method.

To get the most effective use from your Instant Pot, make sure you use recipes that are specifically designed for this type of cooking tool. Make sure you use enough liquid when you're cooking, and don't try to fry anything in it because oil can damage the system.

Keep it simple at the start

It's going to take you a while to familiarize yourself with the variety of functions with which an Instant Pot is equipped. If you are just getting started with your new pot, you need to keep things simple. Rather than trying your hand at a complex recipe, try something easy first, such as boiling eggs, warming up a dish, or your favorite chicken noodle recipe.

Add extra time

When referring to an Instant Pot recipe, you may need to add an extra 10 minutes to the cooking time since the pressure cooker needs time to build up heat and pressure. However, you don't need to add cook time if you're using the slow cooker or sauté options. Because of the time lag involved in both starting and stopping the pressure cooking process, fish and seafood have to be treated with particular care since many of these ingredients can turn either mushy or rubbery if overcooked.

Don't overfill the Instant Pot

A good rule of a thumb is to fill your pot only two-thirds of the way, and if making something that is supposed to rise during cooking, fill it only halfway through. Overfilling the pot may contribute to clogging the valve and will increase the pressure significantly.

Don't use too much liquid

Yes, the Instant Pot needs liquid in order to build up the pressure. However, keep in mind that too much liquid can dilute the flavor and make your meals bland. Unless the recipe calls otherwise, do not use more than 1½ cups of liquid.

Get extra parts

The Instant Pot comes with a stainless steel inner pot. Getting an extra inner pot could help you to prepare two different dishes. Also, if you use the Instant Pot quite often, then you will always have one inner pot available for use while the other is being cleaned in the dishwasher.

You can also cook with different lids. You can get a glass lid, which is similar to a slow cooker lid, and use this lid when you're using the sauté or slow cooker functions. The glass lid cannot be used for the pressure cooking function.

Clean it regularly

Just because it takes less time to cook, does not mean that an Instant Pot doesn't require frequent cleaning. Fortunately, this appliance is very easy to clean, as the inner pot is easily detachable. Make it a habit to clean your Instant Pot after each use.

If you follow the low carb diet, learning to prepare low carb recipes is an important step towards achieving your goals. The 100 easy and delicious low carb Instant Pot recipes in this book will hopefully have you excited about eating well. You will notice a number of improvements in your health and your life. Enjoy the weight loss and the food that makes it easy.

CHAPTER THREE

Breakfast

Eggs with Cheddar and Jalapenos

Yield: 6 servings
Preparation Time: 15 minutes
Cooking Time: 7 minutes
Total Time: 22 minutes
Ingredients:
¼ teaspoon garlic salt
½ teaspoon lemon pepper seasoning
12 eggs
4 Jalapeno peppers, chopped
1 cup sharp Cheddar cheese, shredded
1½ cups water

Directions:
1. Pour the water into your Instant Pot. Lower a steamer trivet.

2. In a bowl, beat the eggs and season with lemon pepper seasoning and garlic salt. Stir in the chopped jalapenos and Cheddar.

3. Divide the egg mixture among 6 sealable jars.

4. Place a lid on top of each jar, but do not tighten.

5. Place the jars on the trivet.

6. Close the lid, select MANUAL, and cook at high pressure for 7 minutes.

7. Release the pressure naturally for 10 minutes. Quick release the remaining pressure.

8. Serve warm.

Nutritional Information (Per Serving)

Calories: 207
Fat: 15.1 g
Net Carbohydrates: 1.4 g
Protein: 15.9 g

Spicy Diced Eggs

Yield: 4 servings
Preparation Time: 10 minutes
Cooking Time: 4 minutes
Total Time: 14 minutes
Ingredients:
6 eggs
¼ teaspoon smoked paprika
½ teaspoon chili powder
¼ teaspoon cayenne pepper
½ teaspoon garlic powder
¼ teaspoon salt
¼ teaspoon black pepper
¼ teaspoon onion powder
2 tablespoons butter, melt
1½ cups water

Directions:
1. Pour the water into your Instant Pot and lower a steamer trivet.

2. Grease a baking dish with cooking spray and crack the eggs into it. Make sure not to break the yolks.

3. Cover the dish with foil and place in the Instant Pot.

4. Close the lid, select MANUAL, and cook at high pressure for 4 minutes.

5. Do a quick pressure release and transfer the egg mixture to a cutting board.

6. Dice finely and stir in the spices and butter.

7. Serve and enjoy!

Nutritional Information (Per Serving)
Calories: 149
Fat: 12.4 g
Net Carbohydrates: 1.0 g
Protein: 8.5 g

Egg and Mushroom Cups

Yield: 4 servings
Preparation Time: 15 minutes
Cooking Time: 8 minutes
Total Time: 23 minutes
Ingredients:
4 eggs, beaten
½ cup sharp Cheddar cheese, shredded
¼ cup half-and-half
Salt and pepper to taste
1 cup fresh mushrooms, chopped
2 tablespoons fresh cilantro, chopped
½ cup Parmesan cheese, shredded

Directions:
1. In a bowl, add all ingredients except Parmesan cheese and mix well.

2. Divide the egg mixture into 4 (½-pint) hear-proof jars evenly.

3. Place a lid on top of each jar, but do not tighten.

4. In the bottom of your Instant Pot, arrange a steamer trivet and pour 2 cups of water.

5. Place the egg jars on the trivet.

6. Close the lid, select MANUAL, and cook at high pressure for 5 minutes.

7. Meanwhile, preheat the broiler of oven.

8. When the cooking is complete, do a quick pressure release.

9. Open the lid and transfer the jars onto a counter.

10. Uncover the jars and sprinkle with Parmesan cheese evenly.

11. Broil in the oven for 2–3 minutes or until the cheese is melted.

12. Serve warm.

Nutritional Information (Per Serving)
Calories: 226
Fat: 16.3 g
Net Carbohydrates: 2.3 g
Protein: 17.6 g

Eggs in Bell Pepper Cups

Yield: 4 servings
Preparation Time: 15 minutes
Cooking Time: 4 minutes
Total Time: 19 minutes
Ingredients:
4 bell peppers
4 eggs
Salt and pepper to taste
4 tablespoons mozzarella cheese, freshly grated

Directions:
1. With a sharp knife, cut the bell peppers ends to form about 1½-inch high cup. Remove the seeds completely.

2. Carefully, crack 1 eggs in each bell pepper cup. Cover each bell peppers with a piece of foil.

3. In the bottom of Instant Pot, arrange a steamer trivet and pour ½ cup of water.

4. Place the bell peppers on top of the trivet.

5. Close the lid, select MANUAL, and cook at low pressure for 4 minutes.

6. When the cooking is complete, do a quick pressure release.

7. Open the lid and transfer the bell pepper cups onto serving plates.

8. Sprinkle with salt, pepper, and cheese and serve.

Nutritional Information (Per Serving)
Calories: 181
Fat: 9.7 g
Net Carbohydrates: 8.8 g
Protein: 14.7 g

Cheesy Spinach Egg Cups

Yield: 4 servings
Preparation Time: 15 minutes
Cooking Time: 8 minutes
Total Time: 23 minutes
Ingredients:

6 eggs

1 tomato, chopped

½ cup shredded Mozzarella cheese

½ cup crumbled Feta cheese

2 tablespoons butter, melt

¼ teaspoon garlic powder

Salt and pepper to taste

1 cup baby spinach, packed

1½ cups Water

Directions:

1. Pour the water into the Instant Pot and lower the trivet.

2. Whisk the eggs in a bowl and season with garlic powder and some salt and pepper. Stir in the chopped tomato, Mozzarella, Feta cheese, and butter.

3. Grease 4 ramekins with some cooking spray. Divide the spinach among them.

4. Pour the egg mixture over the spinach.

5. Place the ramekins on top of the trivet.

6. Close the lid, select MANUAL, and cook at high pressure for 8 minutes.

7. When the cooking is complete, do a quick pressure release.

8. Serve and enjoy!

Nutritional Information (Per Serving)
Calories: 210
Fat: 17 g
Net Carbohydrates: 2.1 g

Protein: 12.3 g

Kale Casserole

Yield: 4 servings
Preparation Time: 15 minutes
Cooking Time: 20 minutes
Total Time: 35 minutes
Ingredients:
6 eggs
½ cup heavy cream
Salt and pepper to taste
1 cup Cheddar cheese, shredded
2½ cups fresh kale, trimmed and chopped
1 small yellow onion, chopped
1 teaspoon Herbs de Provence

Directions:
1. In a large bowl, add eggs, heavy cream, salt, and pepper and beat until well combined.
2. Add remaining ingredients and mix well.
3. Place the mixture into a baking dish evenly.
4. In the bottom of your Instant Pot, arrange a steamer trivet and pour 1 cup of water.
5. Place the baking dish on top of the trivet.
6. Close the lid, select MANUAL, and cook at high pressure for 20 minutes.
7. When the cooking is complete, use a natural pressure release.
8. Serve warm.

Nutritional Information (Per Serving)
Calories: 288
Fat: 21.5 g
Net Carbohydrates: 6.3 g

Protein: 7.1 g

Spinach and Tomato Frittata

Yield: 8 servings
Preparation Time: 20 minutes
Cooking Time: 20 minutes
Total Time: 40 minutes
Ingredients:
12 large eggs
½ cup unsweetened almond milk
Salt and pepper to taste
3 cups fresh spinach
1 cup tomato, seeded and chopped
3 large scallions, sliced
4 tomato slices
¼ cup Parmesan cheese, shredded

Directions:
1. Lightly, grease a 1½ quart casserole dish that will fit in your Instant Pot. Keep aside.
2. In a large bowl, add eggs, milk, salt, and pepper and beat until well combined.
3. In the bottom of the prepared casserole dish, place spinach, chopped tomato, and scallions and stir to combine.
4. Top with the egg mixture and stir to combine.
5. Arrange tomatoes slices on top and sprinkle with Parmesan cheese.
6. In the bottom of Instant Pot, arrange a steamer trivet and pour 1 cup of water.
7. Fold a larger piece of foil in thirds to make a sling. Arrange the foil sling on top of steamer trivet.
8. Place the casserole dish on the foil.

9. Close the lid, select MANUAL, and cook at high pressure for 20 minutes.

10. When the cooking is complete, do a natural pressure release for 10 minutes. Quick release the remaining pressure.

11. Serve warm.

Nutritional Information (Per Serving)
Calories: 162
Fat: 10.5 g
Net Carbohydrates: 2.4 g
Protein: 14 g

Broccoli, Ham and Pepper Frittata

Yield: 4 servings
Preparation Time: 15 minutes
Cooking Time: 20 minutes
Total Time: 35 minutes
Ingredients:
8 ounces ham, cubed
2 cups frozen broccoli
1 cup half and half
½ teaspoon salt
1 cup green pepper, sliced
4 eggs
1 cup shredded cheddar cheese
1 teaspoon ground pepper

Directions:
1. Grease a round baking dish with cooking spray. Add the green pepper, ham, and broccoli.
2. In a bowl, whisk together the eggs, cream, pepper, and salt.
3. Pour the egg mixture over the veggies, and add the cheddar cheese on top.
4. Cover the dish with a foil.
5. Add 2 cups of water into the Instant Pot, then place a steamer trivet. Place the baking dish on the trivet.
6. Close the lid, select MANUAL, and cook at high pressure for 20 minutes.
7. When the cooking is complete, do a natural pressure release for 10 minutes. Quick release the remaining pressure.
8. Uncover the dish and enjoy!

Nutritional Information (Per Serving)
Calories: 369
Fat: 25.8 g
Net Carbohydrates: 7.4 g

Protein: 25.3 g

Mexican Frittata

Yield: 4 servings
Preparation Time: 15 minutes
Cooking Time: 20 minutes
Total Time: 35 minutes
Ingredients:
4 eggs
1 cup half & half
½ teaspoon cumin
1 cup shredded Mexican cheese blend
1 red chili, chopped
¼ cup cilantro, chopped
Salt and pepper to taste
2 cups water

Directions:
1. Pour the water into your Instant Pot and lower the trivet.
2. In a bowl, whisk the eggs along with the half & half, cumin, and half of the cheese. Season with some salt and pepper and stir in the chopped chili and cilantro.
3. Grease a round baking dish with cooking spray, and pour the egg mixture into it.
4. Cover the dish with a foil and place on the trivet.
5. Close the lid, select MANUAL, and cook at high pressure for 20 minutes.
6. When the cooking is complete, do a natural pressure release for 10 minutes. Quick release the remaining pressure.
7. Uncover the dish and sprinkle the rest of the cheese on top.
8. Serve and enjoy!

Nutritional Information (Per Serving)
Calories: 150
Fat: 13.7 g
Net Carbohydrates: 4.1 g
Protein: 9.1 g

Veggie Quiche

Yield: 6 servings
Preparation Time: 20 minutes
Cooking Time: 30 minutes
Total Time: 50 minutes
Ingredients:
½ cup unsweetened almond milk
½ cup almond flour
8 large eggs
Salt and pepper to taste
1 cup tomato, chopped
1 medium zucchini, chopped
1 medium green bell pepper, seeded and chopped
1½ cups mozzarella cheese, shredded

Directions:
1. In a heatproof bowl, add milk, flour, eggs, salt, and pepper and beat until well combined.
2. Add vegetables and 1 cup of cheese and stir to combine.
3. In the bottom of Instant Pot, arrange a steamer trivet and pour 1 cup of water.
4. Cover the bowl with a piece of foil and place on top of the trivet.
5. Close the lid, select MANUAL, and cook at high pressure for 30 minutes.
6. When the cooking is complete, do a natural pressure release for 10 minutes. Quick release the remaining pressure.

7. Serve immediately.

Nutritional Information (Per Serving)
Calories: 149
Fat: 9.5 g
Net Carbohydrates: 3.9 g
Protein: 11.8 g

Beef and Ham Quiche

Yield: 6 servings
Preparation Time: 15 minutes
Cooking Time: 30 minutes
Total Time: 45 minutes
Ingredients:
½ cup unsweetened almond milk
6 large eggs
Pepper to taste
1 cup ground beef, cooked
4 bacon slices, cooked and crumbled
½ cup ham, chopped
1 cup Parmesan cheese, shredded
2 scallions, chopped

Directions:
1. Lightly, grease a soufflé dish that will fit in the Instant Pot. Keep aside.
2. In a bowl, add almond milk, eggs, and pepper and beat until well combined.
3. In another bowl, mix together remaining ingredients.
4. Transfer the meat mixture into the prepared soufflé dish. Pour the egg mixture on top and gently, stir to combine.
5. Cover the soufflé dish with a piece of foil.

6. In the bottom of Instant Pot, arrange a steamer trivet and pour 1½ cups of water.

7. Fold a larger piece of foil in thirds to make a sling. Place the foil sling on the trivet.

8. Place the soufflé dish on the sling.

9. Close the lid, select MANUAL, and cook at high pressure for 30 minutes.

10. When the cooking is complete, do a quick pressure release.

11. Serve warm.

Nutritional Information (Per Serving)
Calories: 325
Fat: 20.3 g
Net Carbohydrates: 1.7 g
Protein: 32 g

Bacon and Sausage Omelet

Yield: 6 servings
Preparation Time: 20 minutes
Cooking Time: 20 minutes
Total Time: 40 minutes
Ingredients:
6 small sausage links, sliced
½ onion, diced
6 eggs
6 bacon slices, cooked and crumbled
⅓ cup milk
Salt and pepper to taste
1½ cups water

Directions:
1. Pour the water into your Instant Pot. Lower a trivet.
2. In a bowl, beat the eggs along with the milk and some salt and pepper. Stir in the sliced sausage, crumbled bacon, and onion.
3. Grease a baking dish with some cooking spray and pour the egg mixture into it.
4. Place the dish on the trivet.
5. Close the lid, select MANUAL, and cook at high pressure for 20 minutes.
6. When the cooking is complete, use a natural pressure release.

Nutritional Information (Per Serving)
Calories: 226
Fat: 17.1 g
Net Carbohydrates: 2.3 g
Protein: 15 g

Sausage-Crusted Ricotta and Kale Pie

Yield: 8 servings
Preparation Time: 15 minutes
Cooking Time: 25 minutes
Total Time: 40 minutes
Ingredients:
1 pound sausage
½ cup diced onion
½ teaspoon minced garlic
8 cups chopped kale
3 eggs
1 tablespoon olive oil
2 cups Ricotta cheese
¼ cup grated Parmesan cheese
1 cup shredded Mozzarella cheese
¼ teaspoon salt
Pinch of pepper
2 cups water

Directions:
1. Set your Instant Pot to SAUTÉ and heat the olive oil in it.
2. Add the onions and cook for a few minutes.
3. Stir in the garlic and sauté for one more minute.
4. Add the kale and cook until it just becomes wilted. Transfer the kale to a plate.
5. In a bowl, beat the eggs along with the salt and pepper. Stir in Ricotta, Parmesan, and Mozzarella cheese.
6. Grease a baking dish that can fit into the Instant Pot with some cooking spray.
7. Roll out the sausage and press it into the bottom of the dish.
8. Arrange the kale and onion mixture on top of the sausage and pour over the cheesy eggs. Cover with a foil.

9. Pour the water into the pot and lower the trivet. Place the baking dish on the trivet.

10. Close the lid, select MANUAL, and cook at high pressure for 25 minutes.

11. When the cooking is complete, use a natural pressure release.

12. Serve and enjoy!

Nutritional Information (Per Serving)
Calories: 374
Fat: 25.8 g
Net Carbohydrates: 10.1 g
Protein: 24.4 g

Cream Cheese Pancakes

Yield: 2 servings
Preparation Time: 5 minutes
Cooking Time: 10 minutes
Total Time: 15 minutes
Ingredients:
4 eggs
½ teaspoon cinnamon
4 ounces cream cheese
2 teaspoon Swerve
1 tablespoon butter

Directions:
1. Place everything, except for the butter, in a blender. Blend until smooth.
2. Melt 1 teaspoon of the butter in your Instant Pot on SAUTÉ.
3. Pour half of the pancake batter and cook for 3 minutes.
4. Add another teaspoon of batter on top, and flip over. Cook for 1–2 minutes more.
5. Repeat with the other pancake.
6. Serve and enjoy!

Nutritional Information (Per Serving)
Calories: 376
Fat: 34.3 g
Net Carbohydrates: 7.4 g
Protein: 15.4 g

CHAPTER FOUR

Poultry

BBQ Chicken Thighs

Yield: 4 servings
Preparation Time: 15 minutes
Cooking Time: 15 minutes
Total Time: 30 minutes
Ingredients:
2 tablespoons olive oil
1 onion, chopped
1 pound chicken thighs
1 garlic clove, minced
2 tablespoons tomato paste
1 tablespoon soy sauce
1 cup plus 2 tablespoons water
1½ tablespoons arrowroot
¼ teaspoon salt
¼ teaspoon pepper

Directions:
1. Heat the oil in your Instant Pot on SAUTÉ. Sauté the onions for a couple of minutes.

2. Add garlic and cook for 30–60 seconds, until fragrant.

3. Whisk in 1 cup of water with the tomato paste and soy sauce. Add the chicken thighs.

4. Close the lid, select MANUAL, and cook at high pressure for 10 minutes.

5. Do a quick pressure release and transfer the thighs to a plate.

6. Add the remaining ingredients to the Instant Pot and whisk to combine.

7. Cook on SAUTÉ until the sauce thickens.

8. Return the chicken to the pot and coat well.

9. Serve and enjoy!

Nutritional Information (Per Serving)
Calories: 323
Fat: 24.1 g
Net Carbohydrates: 4.1 g
Protein: 21.1 g

Stuffed Chicken Breast

Yield: 4 servings
Preparation Time: 20 minutes
Cooking Time: 25 minutes
Total Time: 45 minutes
Ingredients:
2 (6-ounce) boneless, skinless chicken breasts
Salt and pepper to taste
4 thin prosciutto slices
4 thin provolone cheese slices
16 fresh basil leaves
1 tablespoon olive oil
3 tablespoons butter, divided
½ cup onion, diced
2 cups chicken broth, divided
1 teaspoon balsamic vinegar
2 tablespoons fresh parsley, minced

Directions:
1. Butterfly each chicken breast horizontally, then carefully, open each one in half.

2. With a meat mallet, pound each breast into ¼-inch thickness.

3. Season each chicken breast with salt and pepper evenly.

4. Arrange chicken breasts onto a smooth surface, cut side up.

5. Place 2 prosciutto slices in each chicken breast, followed by 2 provolone cheese slices and 8 basil leaves.

6. Roll each chicken breast lengthwise and with kitchen twine, tie together.

7. Place the oil and 1 tablespoon of butter in the Instant Pot and select SAUTÉ. Add the chicken rolls and sear for about 2 minutes per side.

8. Press CANCEL and transfer chicken rolls onto a plate.

9. In the bottom of Instant Pot, arrange a steamer trivet and pour 1 cup of broth.

10. Place the chicken rolls on top of the trivet.

11. Close the lid, select POULTRY, and cook for 8 minutes.

12. When the cooking is complete, do a natural pressure release for 5 minutes. Quick release the remaining pressure.

13. Open the lid and transfer chicken onto a plate to cool for 5–10 minutes.

14. Remove the trivet from Instant Pot and drain the broth. With paper towels, pat dry the pot.

15. Place 1 tablespoon of butter in the Instant Pot and select SAUTÉ. Add the onion and cook for 4–5 minutes.

16. Add remaining broth, vinegar, salt, and pepper and simmer for 3–5 minutes or until desired thickness of sauce.

17. Add remaining butter and parsley and stir to combine.

18. Meanwhile, cut each chicken roll into ½-inch slices.

19. Press CANCEL and pour sauce over chicken slices.

20. Serve immediately.

Nutritional Information (Per Serving)
Calories: 294
Fat: 23 g
Net Carbohydrates: 1.6 g
Protein: 20 g

Chicken and Broccoli

Yield: 4 servings
Preparation Time: 15 minutes
Cooking Time: 23 minutes
Total Time: 38 minutes
Ingredients:
1 tablespoon olive oil
2 (4-ounce) skinless, boneless chicken breasts
Salt and pepper to taste
1 small yellow onion, chopped
1 garlic clove, minced
1¼ cups chicken broth
1½ tablespoons arrowroot starch
3½ tablespoons water, divided
½ cup Cheddar cheese, shredded
2 ounces cream cheese, cubed
2 cups small broccoli florets

Directions:
1. Place the oil in the Instant Pot and select SAUTÉ. Add the chicken breasts and cook for 4–5 minutes.
2. With a slotted spoon, transfer the chicken breasts to a plate.
3. In the pot, add onion and cook for 2–3 minutes.
4. Add garlic and cook for about 1 minute.
5. Press CANCEL and stir in the cooked chicken and chicken broth.
6. Close the lid, select MANUAL, and cook at high pressure for 5 minutes.
7. When the cooking is complete, do a quick pressure release.
8. Open the lid and with tongs, transfer chicken breasts onto a cutting board.
9. With a sharp knife, cut chicken into desired sized pieces.

10. Meanwhile, in a small bowl, dissolve arrowroot starch in 1½ tablespoons of water.

11. Set the Instant Pot to SAUTÉ and add the arrowroot mixture, stirring continuously.

12. Add Cheddar cheese and cream cheese and cook until melted completely, stirring continuously.

13. Meanwhile, in a large microwave-safe bowl, add broccoli and 2 tablespoons of water and microwave on High for 3–4 minutes.

14. Add chopped chicken and broccoli to the Instant Pot and stir well.

15. Simmer for 4–5 minutes.

16. Press CANCEL and serve hot.

Nutritional Information (Per Serving)
Calories: 253
Fat: 15.7 g
Net Carbohydrates: 6.7 g
Protein: 20.3 g

Butter Chicken

Yield: 8 servings
Preparation Time: 15 minutes
Cooking Time: 15 minutes
Total Time: 30 minutes
Ingredients:
2 (14-ounce) cans diced tomatoes with liquid
1 tablespoon garlic, chopped
2 jalapeño peppers, seeded and chopped
½ cup butter
10 (4-ounce) skinless, boneless chicken thighs, cubed
1 tablespoon paprika
¼ teaspoon cayenne pepper
2 teaspoons ground cumin

1 teaspoon ground coriander

½ teaspoon ground turmeric

¾ cup plain Greek yogurt, whipped

¾ cup cream

Salt to taste

2 tablespoons arrowroot starch

2 tablespoons water

¼ cup fresh cilantro, chopped

Directions:

1. In a food processor, add tomatoes, garlic, and jalapeño peppers and pulse until smooth. Keep aside.

2. Place the butter in the Instant Pot and select SAUTÉ. Add the chicken pieces and cook for about 5 minutes or until browned. Transfer the chicken into a bowl.

3. In the pot, add spices and cook for about 1 minute.

4. Press CANCEL and stir in cooked chicken, yogurt, cream, tomato mixture, and salt.

5. Close the lid, select MANUAL, and cook at high pressure for 5 minutes.

6. When the cooking is complete, use a natural pressure release.

7. Meanwhile in a small bowl, dissolve arrowroot starch in water.

8. Remove the lid and select SAUTÉ.

9. Add arrowroot starch mixture, stirring continuously and cook for 3–4 minutes.

10. Press CANCEL and serve hot with the garnishing of cilantro.

Nutritional Information (Per Serving)
Calories: 343
Fat: 18.6 g
Net Carbohydrates: 7.7 g
Protein: 34.5g

Chicken with Salsa

Yield: 4 servings
Preparation Time: 15 minutes
Cooking Time: 20 minutes
Total Time: 35 minutes
Ingredients:
4 (6-ounce) skinless, boneless frozen chicken breasts
1 cup sugar-free tomato sauce
1 cup mild salsa
3 tablespoons fresh lime juice
Salt and pepper to taste
1 cup mozzarella cheese, grated

Directions:
1. In the Instant Pot, place all ingredients except cheese and mix.
2. Close the lid, select MANUAL, and cook at high pressure for 12 minutes.
3. When the cooking is complete, do a quick pressure release.
4. Preheat the broiler of oven.
5. Open the lid and with tongs, transfer the chicken breasts in a greased baking dish.
6. Set the Instant Pot to SAUTÉ and cook for 2–3 minutes or until desired thickness of mixture.
7. Pour sauce over chicken and sprinkle with cheese.
8. Broil for 4–5 minutes.
9. Serve hot.

Nutritional Information (Per Serving)
Calories: 264
Fat: 7.6 g
Net Carbohydrates: 5.4 g
Protein: 41.5 g

Chicken with Bacon and Cream Cheese

Yield: 4 servings
Preparation Time: 10 minutes
Cooking Time: 30 minutes
Total Time: 40 minutes
Ingredients:
1 pound chicken breasts
8 ounces cream cheese
4 ounces shredded Cheddar cheese
8 bacon slices, cooked and crumbled
2 tablespoons arrowroot
1 teaspoon ranch seasoning
1 cup water

Directions:
1. Combine the water, cream cheese, and ranch seasoning inside the Instant Pot.
2. Place the chicken inside and close the lid.
3. Select MANUAL and cook at high pressure for 25 minutes
4. Do a quick pressure release.
5. Shred the chicken with two forks, inside the Instant Pot.
6. Stir in the arrowroot and set the Instant Pot to SAUTÉ. Cook until the sauce thickens.
7. Stir in the remaining ingredients and cook for another minute.
8. Serve and enjoy!

Nutritional Information (Per Serving)
Calories: 649
Fat: 47.9 g
Net Carbohydrates: 2.8 g
Protein: 49.3 g

Chicken Salad

Yield: 8 servings
Preparation Time: 15 minutes
Cooking Time: 15 minutes
Total Time: 30 minutes
Ingredients:
For chicken:
15 ounces tomatoes, diced
½ cup onion, diced
3 garlic cloves, minced
2 tablespoons tomato paste
Salt and pepper to taste
¼ teaspoon coriander
¼ teaspoon cocoa powder
1 teaspoon cumin
1 teaspoon chili powder
2 pounds chicken meat

For Salad:
10 cups torn romaine lettuce
1 cup cilantro, chopped
4 scallions, chopped
2 cups cherry tomatoes, sliced in half
2 cups cubed cheddar cheese
½ cup olives, chopped
2 avocados, diced
Low carb ranch dressing

Directions:
1. Stir all taco ingredients, except the chicken, into an Instant Pot.
2. Place the chicken on top of the ingredients.

3. Close the lid, select MANUAL, and cook at high pressure for 8 minutes.

4. When the cooking is complete, use a natural pressure release.

5. Transfer the chicken to a platter and shred the meat.

6. Place the sauce in a blender and puree for smoothness.

7. Combine all salad ingredients in a bowl. Top with the chicken.

8. Drizzle the sauce over the salad.

9. Serve with ranch dressing.

Nutritional Information (Per Serving)
Calories: 473
Fat: 28.9 g
Net Carbohydrates: 6.6 g
Protein: 42.2 g

Chicken and Cauliflower with White Sauce

Yield: 4 servings
Preparation Time: 15 minutes
Cooking Time: 15 minutes
Total Time: 30 minutes
Ingredients:
1 butter stick
3 cups cauliflower florets
8 ounces cream cheese
2 cups heavy cream
1 tablespoon chopped basil
1 garlic clove, minced
1 pound chicken breasts, cubed

Directions:
1. Place the cauliflower florets in your food processor and pulse until ground.

2. Melt the butter inside the Instant Pot on SAUTÉ. Add the cream cheese and cream and whisk to combine.

3. Stir in the garlic, chicken, basil, and cauliflower rice.

4. Close the lid, select MANUAL, and cook at high pressure for 15 minutes.

5. When the cooking is complete, do a quick pressure release.

Nutritional Information (Per Serving)
Calories: 757
Fat: 67.8 g
Net Carbohydrates: 5.6 g
Protein: 31.4 g

Hungarian Chicken Legs

Yield: 4 servings
Preparation Time: 15 minutes
Cooking Time: 25 minutes
Total Time: 40 minutes
Ingredients:
4 chicken thighs
1 tablespoon olive oil
1 tomato, chopped
2 teaspoons paprika
½ cup sour cream
½ onion, diced
½ cup chicken broth
¼ teaspoon salt
¼ teaspoon black pepper

Directions:
1. Set your Instant Pot to SAUTÉ and heat the olive oil in it.

2. Add the legs and cook for a couple of minutes, until they become golden on all sides. Transfer to a plate.

3. Add the onions to the Instant Pot and sauté until softened. Add the chicken broth and stir in the paprika.

4. Return the chicken to the pot and add tomatoes. Press CANCEL.

5. Close the lid, select MANUAL, and cook at high pressure for 10 minutes.

6. When the cooking is complete, do a quick pressure release.

7. Transfer the chicken to a plate.

8. Whisk the sour cream into the cooking liquid.

9. Drizzle the sauce over the chicken.

10. Serve and enjoy!

Nutritional Information (Per Serving)

Calories: 258
Fat: 19.4 g
Net Carbohydrates: 3.0 g
Protein: 17 g

Roasted Turkey

Yield: 8 servings
Preparation Time: 15 minutes
Cooking Time: 50 minutes
Total Time: 1 hour 5 minutes
Ingredients:
1 (11-pound) whole turkey, necks and gibbets removed
Salt and pepper to taste
3 tablespoons butter
2–3 fresh thyme sprigs
2–3 fresh rosemary sprigs
1 cup chicken broth
2 tablespoons fresh lemon juice

Directions:
1. Season turkey with salt and pepper evenly.
2. Place the butter in the Instant Pot and select SAUTÉ. Add the turkey and cook for 4–5 minutes or until browned.
3. Press CANCEL and transfer turkey onto a tray.
4. Stuff the cavity of turkey with herb sprigs and tie up the legs together.
5. In the Instant Pot, place the turkey and pour broth and lemon juice on top.
6. Close the lid, select MANUAL, and cook at high pressure for 45 minutes.
7. When the cooking is complete, do a natural pressure release for 10 minutes. Quick release the remaining pressure.

8. Open the lid and place turkey onto a cutting board to cool for 15–20 minutes before carving.

9. Slice the turkey and serve.

Nutritional Information (Per Serving)
Calories: 1108
Fat: 35.8 g
Net Carbohydrates: 0.6 g
Protein: 183.5 g

Habanero Turkey

Yield: 6 servings
Preparation Time: 15 minutes
Cooking Time: 15 minutes
Total Time: 30 minutes
Ingredients:
2 pounds turkey breasts, cubed
6 tablespoons habanero sauce
8 ounces cream cheese
1 tablespoon Swerve
½ teaspoon cumin
½ cup tomato puree
1 teaspoon smoked paprika
½ teaspoon basil
Salt and pepper to taste
1½ cups water
8 ounces cheddar cheese
1 cup sour cream

Directions:
1. Add water, turkey, habanero sauce, cream cheese, spices and herbs, tomato puree, and salt to the Instant Pot. Sit to combine well.

2. Close the lid, select MANUAL, and cook at high pressure for 15 minutes.

3. When the cooking is complete, do a natural pressure release for 10 minutes. Quick release the remaining pressure.

4. Add the cheddar cheese and sour cream to the pot. Stir to combine well.

5. Enjoy!

Nutritional Information (Per Serving)
Calories: 637
Fat: 41.5 g
Net Carbohydrates: 7.9 g
Protein: 48.4 g

Tender Whole Chicken

Yield: 8 servings
Preparation Time: 15 minutes
Cooking Time: 35 minutes
Total Time: 50 minutes
Ingredients:
1 4-pound chicken
2 garlic cloves, peeled
2 tablespoons lemon juice
2 tablespoons coconut oil
1½ cups chicken stock
1 teaspoon paprika
1 teaspoon onion powder
¼ teaspoon pepper
¼ teaspoon salt

Directions:
1. In a small bowl, combine the spices. Rub the spice mixture into the chicken.

2. Set your Instant Pot to SAUTÉ and melt the coconut oil in it. Cook the chicken on all sides, until golden brown.

3. Pour the chicken stock and lemon juice over the chicken. Add the garlic and close the lid.

4. Select MANUAL and cook at high pressure for 25 minutes.

5. When the cooking is complete, use a natural pressure release.

Nutritional Information (Per Serving)
Calories: 481
Fat: 22 g
Net Carbohydrates: 0.7 g
Protein: 55.9 g

Tomato Turkey Meatballs

Yield: 4 servings
Preparation Time: 15 minutes
Cooking Time: 10 minutes
Total Time: 25 minutes
Ingredients:
1 pound ground turkey
¼ onion, diced
⅓ cup almond flour
½ cup grated Parmesan cheese
½ teaspoon garlic powder
¼ cup chicken stock
28 ounces canned diced tomatoes
1 tablespoon olive oil
½ teaspoon basil
¼ teaspoon oregano
¼ teaspoon salt
¼ teaspoon pepper

Directions:

1. In a bowl, mix the turkey, onion, almond flour, and Parmesan until well combined.

2. Shape the mixture into small meatballs.

3. Place the remaining ingredients in your Instant Pot and stir to combine.

4. Place the meatballs inside.

5. Close the lid, select MANUAL, and cook at high pressure for 10 minutes.

6. When the cooking is complete, use a natural pressure release.

7. Serve and enjoy!

Nutritional Information (Per Serving)
Calories: 350

Fat: 20.6 g
Net Carbohydrates: 6.9 g
Protein: 38 g

Italian Duck

Yield: 4 servings
Preparation Time: 15 minutes
Cooking Time: 25 minutes
Total Time: 40 minutes
Ingredients:
2 pounds duck breasts, halved
2 garlic cloves, minced
½ cup chopped sun-dried tomatoes
1 cup chopped spinach
2 tablespoons olive oil
½ cup grated Parmesan cheese
½ cup chicken broth
½ tablespoon Italian seasoning
¼ teaspoon salt
¾ cup heavy cream
Pinch of pepper

Directions:
1. In a small bowl, combine the oil and spices. Rub the spice mixture into the meat.

2. Set your Instant Pot to SAUTÉ and add the duck. Cook on all sides until golden.

3. Add the chicken broth. Close the lid, select MANUAL, and cook at high pressure for 4 minutes.

4. When the cooking is complete, do a quick pressure release.

5. Open the lid and stir in the rest of the ingredients.

6. Close the lid, select MANUAL, and cook at high pressure for 5 minutes.

7. When the cooking is complete, do a quick pressure release.

Nutritional Information (Per Serving)
Calories: 490
Fat: 28.1 g
Net Carbohydrates: 2.6 g
Protein: 45.3 g

Roasted Duck

Yield: 3 servings
Preparation Time: 15 minutes
Cooking Time: 30 minutes
Total Time: 45 minutes
Ingredients:
1 (3½-pound) duck
Salt and pepper to taste
2 tablespoons butter
1 lemon, halved
2 sprigs fresh rosemary
½ cup chicken broth

Directions:
1. With a fork, prick the skin of the duck.
2. Season the body and cavity of duck with salt and pepper.
3. Stuff the cavity of duck with lemon halves and rosemary sprigs and tie the legs together.
4. Place the butter in Instant Pot and select SAUTÉ. Add the duck and cook for 4–5 minutes or until browned from all sides.
5. Press CANCEL and remove grease from the pot.
6. Add broth into Instant Pot.
7. Close the lid, select MANUAL, and cook at high pressure for 25 minutes.
8. When the cooking is complete, use a natural pressure release.
9. Open the lid and transfer the duck to a cutting board.
10. Cut into desired sized pieces and serve.

Nutritional Information (Per Serving)
Calories: 279
Fat: 17.1 g
Net Carbohydrates: 0.7 g
Protein: 28.7 g

CHAPTER FIVE

Meats

Chuck Roast

Yield: 6 servings
Preparation Time: 15 minutes
Cooking Time: 35 minutes
Total Time: 50 minutes
Ingredients:
For Rub:
2 tablespoons coffee, finely ground
1 tablespoon cacao powder
1 tablespoon smoked paprika
1 teaspoon ground ginger
1 teaspoon red chili powder
1 teaspoon red pepper flakes, crushed
Salt and pepper to taste
2 pounds beef chuck roast, trimmed and cut into 1½-inch cubes

For Sauce:
1 cup beef broth
½ cup brewed coffee
1 medium yellow onion, chopped
2 tablespoons fresh lemon juice
Salt and pepper to taste

Directions:
1. For rub: in a small bowl, mix together all ingredients except roast.
2. Rub chuck roast with the rub mixture generously.

3. For sauce: in a food processor, add all ingredients and pulse until smooth.

4. In the Instant Pot, place roast and top with the sauce.

5. Close the lid, select MEAT/STEW, and cook for 35 minutes.

6. When the cooking is complete, use a natural pressure release.

7. Open the lid and transfer the roast onto a platter. With 2 forks, shred the meat.

8. Top with cooking liquid and serve.

Nutritional Information (Per Serving)
Calories: 573
Fat: 42.8 g
Net Carbohydrates: 2.3 g
Protein: 41.1 g

Beef Short Ribs

Yield: 8 servings
Preparation Time: 15 minutes
Cooking Time: 1 hour
Total Time: 1 hour 15 minutes
Ingredients:
½ cup almond flour
Salt and pepper to taste
3¼ pounds beef short ribs
3 tablespoons unsalted butter, divided
1 small yellow onion, chopped
2 garlic cloves, minced
1 tablespoon fresh rosemary, chopped
½ cup beef broth

Directions:
1. In a large bowl, mix together almond flour, salt, and pepper.

2. Add beef ribs and coat with the flour mixture generously. Shake off excess mixture.

3. Place 1 tablespoon of butter in the Instant Pot and select SAUTÉ. Add the ribs and cook for 4–5 minutes or until browned completely.

4. Transfer the beef ribs into a bowl.

5. Add remaining butter and onion and cook for 2–3 minutes.

6. Add garlic and rosemary and cook for about 1 minute.

7. Stir in broth and water and cook for about 1 minute.

8. Press CANCEL and stir in the beef ribs.

9. Close the lid, select MANUAL, and cook at high pressure for 50 minutes.

10. When the cooking is complete, do a quick pressure release.

11. Remove the lid and transfer ribs onto a serving platter.

12. Top with cooking liquid and serve.

Nutritional Information (Per Serving)
Calories: 434
Fat: 22 g
Net Carbohydrates: 1.2 g
Protein: 54.1 g

Feta Meatloaf

Yield: 6 servings
Preparation Time: 10 minutes
Cooking Time: 23 minutes
Total Time: 25 minutes
Ingredients:
1 small yellow onion, chopped roughly
6–8 garlic cloves, chopped
2 teaspoons fresh rosemary
2 teaspoons fresh marjoram
Salt and pepper to taste

2 pounds ground beef

¼ cup feta cheese, crumbled

Directions:

1. In a food processor, add onion and pule until finely chopped.

2. Place chopped onion in a paper towel and squeeze out all the liquid.

3. Return the onion to the food processor with garlic, herbs, salt, and pepper and pulse until garlic is minced.

4. Add ground beef and pulse until well combined.

5. Place mixture into a loaf pan and press firmly.

6.Cover the loaf pan with a piece of foil tightly and with a fork, poke a few vent holes in the foil.

7. In the bottom of Instant Pot, arrange a steamer trivet and pour 1 cup of water.

8. Arrange the meatloaf on top of the trivet.

9. Close the lid, select MANUAL, and cook at high pressure for 20 minutes.

10. When the cooking is complete, use a natural pressure release.

11. Preheat the broiler of oven.

12. Remove loaf pan and place onto a wire rack to cool for about 15 minutes.

13. Carefully, remove meatloaf from pan and transfer onto a broiler pan.

14. Broil for 2–3 minutes.

15. Remove from oven and immediately, top with feta cheese.

16. Cut into desired sized slices and serve.

Nutritional Information (Per Serving)
Calories: 310
Fat: 10.9 g
Net Carbohydrates: 2.5 g
Protein: 47.2 g

French Dip

Yield: 6 servings
Preparation Time: 10 minutes
Cooking Time: 45 minutes
Total Time: 55 minutes
Ingredients:
2 pounds beef chuck roast, trimmed of fat
4 cloves garlic
½ teaspoon pepper corns
Lettuce cups to serve
4 tablespoons soy sauce
¾ teaspoon dried rosemary
¾ teaspoon dried thyme
¾ teaspoon garlic powder
1½ cups water

Directions:
1. Add all the ingredients except lettuce cups to the Instant Pot.
2. Cover, select MEAT/STEW, and cook for 45 minutes.
3. When the cooking is complete, use a natural pressure release.
4. Remove the roast. When cool enough to handle, shred with a pair of forks.
5. Serve meat in lettuce cups, with cooking liquid served in cups or bowls to dip.

Nutritional Information (Per Serving)
Calories: 569
Fat: 42.1 g
Net Carbohydrates: 3.9 g
Protein: 39.8 g

Herb Meatloaf

Yield: 6 servings
Preparation Time: 15 minutes
Cooking Time: 40 minutes
Total Time: 55 minutes
Ingredients:
3 tablespoons olive oil
1 teaspoon oregano
2 teaspoons thyme
1 teaspoon rosemary
½ teaspoon parsley
2 pounds ground beef
¼ teaspoon pepper
2 eggs
3 tablespoons almond flour
1 teaspoon garlic salt
1½ cups water

Directions:
1. Pour the water into your Instant Pot and lower the trivet.
2. Grease a loaf pan that fits inside your Instant Pot with the olive oil.
3. Place the remaining ingredients in a large bowl. Mix with your hands until well incorporated. Transfer the mixture to the loaf pan and press firmly.
4. Place the loaf pan on the trivet and close the lid.
5. Set the Instant Pot to MANUAL and cook at high pressure for 30 minutes.
6. When the cooking is complete, do a natural pressure release for 10 minutes. Quick release the remaining pressure.

Nutritional Information (Per Serving)
Calories: 531

Fat: 46.3 g

Net Carbohydrates: 0.7 g

Protein: 26.2 g

Tender Beef Pot Roast

Yield: 6 servings

Preparation Time: 15 minutes

Cooking Time: 45 minutes

Total Time: 60 minutes

Ingredients:

1 onion, sliced

2 teaspoons minced garlic

2½ pounds beef roast

2 tablespoons sugar-free steak sauce

2 celery stalks, chopped

1 bell pepper, chopped

2 tablespoons olive oil

1 cup beef broth

1 tablespoon balsamic vinegar

1½ tablespoons Italian seasoning

Directions:

1. Heat 1 tablespoon of olive oil in your Instant Pot on SAUTÉ.

2. Add the beef and sear it on all sides until browned, about 5 minutes in total. Transfer to a plate.

3. Heat the remaining oil in the Instant Pot and add the onions, celery, and pepper. Cook for a few minutes, until soft.

4. Add garlic and cook for 30 seconds.

5. Return the meat to the pot.

6. In a bowl, whisk together the broth, vinegar, and Italian Seasoning. Pour the mixture over the beef.

7. Close the lid, select MANUAL, and cook at high pressure for 40 minutes.

8. When the cooking is complete, use a natural pressure release.

9. Serve and enjoy!

Nutritional Information (Per Serving)
Calories: 603
Fat: 40.4 g
Net Carbohydrates: 4.5 g
Protein: 51.7 g

Mexican Beef

Yield: 6 servings
Preparation Time: 15 minutes
Cooking Time: 40 minutes
Total Time: 55 minutes
Ingredients:
3 pounds boneless beef short ribs, cubed
2 teaspoons salt
1 medium onion, thinly sliced
6 garlic cloves, peeled and smashed
½ cup bone broth
Ground black pepper
2 radishes, sliced
1 tablespoon chili powder
1 tablespoon butter
1 tablespoon tomato paste
½ cup tomato salsa
½ teaspoon fish sauce
½ cup minced cilantro

Directions:

1. Heat the butter in your Instant Pot on SAUTÉ. Add the onion, and cook until soft.

2. Add the beef, and cook until browned.

3. Include the rest of the ingredients. Mix to combine.

4. Close the lid, select MANUAL, and cook at high pressure for 35 minutes.

5. When the cooking is complete, use a natural pressure release.

6. Season to taste and then serve.

Nutritional Information (Per Serving)
Calories: 438
Fat: 25 g
Net Carbohydrates: 5.6 g
Protein: 43.7 g

Knorr Demi-Glace Brisket

Yield: 4 servings
Preparation Time: 10 minutes
Cooking Time: 70 minutes
Total Time: 80 minutes
Ingredients:
2 tablespoons olive oil
2 pounds beef brisket
1 onion, chopped
2 celery stalks, chopped
2 garlic cloves, minced
2 bay leaves
1¼ cups beef broth
2 tablespoons Knorr Demi-glace sauce
1 tablespoon Worcestershire sauce
½ teaspoon salt
½ teaspoon black pepper

Directions:
1. Season the brisket with salt and pepper.
2. Heat 1 tablespoon of olive oil in your Instant Pot on SAUTÉ and add the beef. Sear for about 2 minutes per side. Transfer to a plate.
3. Heat the other tablespoon of oil and add the onions and celery. Cook until soft. Stir in the garlic and cook for another minute.
4. Return the beef to the pot and add the bay leaves.
5. In a bowl, whisk together the broth and sauces and pour the mixture over the beef.
6. Close the lid, select MEAT/STEW, and cook for 1 hour.
7. When the cooking is complete, use a natural pressure release.
8. Serve and enjoy!

Nutritional Information (Per Serving)

Calories: 735
Fat: 58.3 g
Net Carbohydrates: 6.1 g
Protein: 45.8 g

Pork Carnitas

Yield: 4 servings
Preparation Time: 15 minutes
Cooking Time: 55 minutes
Total Time: 70 minutes
Ingredients:
2 pounds pork shoulder
1 onion, chopped
1 teaspoon cumin
Juice of 2 limes
1 teaspoon oregano
2 cups beef broth
1 tablespoon olive oil
½ cup water
1 Jalapeno, diced
2 garlic cloves, minced

Directions:
1. Set the Instant Pot to SAUTÉ and heat the oil in it.
2. Sear the pork on all sides, until browned. Transfer the seared pork to a plate.
3. Add the onions and garlic and cook for 2 minutes. Stir in the remaining ingredients.
4. Return the pork to the pot and close the lid.
5. Set the Instant Pot to MANUAL and cook on HIGH for 30 minutes.
6. Let the pressure drop on its own, about 20 minutes.

7. Shred the pork inside the pot with two forks.

8. Set the pot to SAUTÉ and cook with the lid off until the sauce thickens a bit.

9. Serve and enjoy!

Nutritional Information (Per Serving)
Calories: 652
Fat: 50.4 g
Net Carbohydrates: 5.1 g
Protein: 41.1 g

Balsamic-Glazed Pork Loin

Yield: 4 servings
Preparation Time: 15 minutes
Cooking Time: 65 minutes
Total Time: 80 minutes
Ingredients:
1 garlic clove, minced
1 teaspoon sage
2 pounds pork loin
½ cup beef broth
½ teaspoon pepper

Glaze:
1 tablespoon arrowroot
¼ cup balsamic vinegar
½ cup Swerve
2 tablespoons coconut aminos
½ cup water

Directions:
1. Rub the pork with the sage, pepper, and garlic. Place it inside the Instant Pot and pour the broth over.

2. Close the lid, select MANUAL, and cook at high pressure for 1 hour.

3. When the cooking is complete, do a natural pressure release for 10 minutes. Quick release the remaining pressure.

4. Meanwhile, whisk together the glaze ingredients.

5. You can either brush the mixture over the pork loin and sear on SAUTÉ for a few minutes, or shred the meat, pour the sauce over and cook on SAUTÉ for 2–3 minutes.

Nutritional Information (Per Serving)
Calories: 568
Fat: 31.8 g
Net Carbohydrates: 12.5 g
Protein: 42.8 g

French Onion Pork Chops

Yield: 4 servings
Preparation Time: 10 minutes
Cooking Time: 20 minutes
Total Time: 30 minutes
Ingredients:
4 pork chops
10 ounces French onion soup
½ cup sour cream
1 cup chicken broth

Directions:

1. Place the pork chops in the Instant Pot and pour the broth over.

2. Close the lid, select MANUAL, and cook at high pressure for 12 minutes.

3. When the cooking is complete, use a natural pressure release.

4. Whisk together the sour cream and French onion soup and pour the mixture over the pork.

5. Set the Instant Pot to SAUTÉ and cook for about 6–8 minutes.

6. Serve and enjoy!

Nutritional Information (Per Serving)
Calories: 365
Fat: 26.9 g
Net Carbohydrates: 6.9 g
Protein: 21.5 g

Pork Ribs

Yield: 8 servings
Preparation Time: 15 minutes
Cooking Time: 40 minutes
Total Time: 55 minutes
Ingredients:
2 garlic cloves, minced
1 teaspoon dried thyme, crushed
1 teaspoon smoked paprika
½ teaspoon ground cumin
½ teaspoon ground coriander
¼ teaspoon ground allspice
Salt and pepper to taste
2½ pounds boneless pork ribs
1 cup chicken broth
1 cup tomato sauce
2 tablespoons fresh lemon juice
2 teaspoons mustard powder
2 tablespoons olive oil
1 medium yellow onion, sliced

Directions:
1. In a large bowl, mix together garlic, thyme, and spices.
2. Add the pork ribs and coat with the spice mixture generously.
3. In another small bowl, mix together broth, tomato sauce, lemon juice, and mustard.
4. Place the oil in the Instant Pot and select SAUTÉ. Add the onion and cook for 4–5 minutes.
5. Press CANCEL and place the ribs over onion and top with the broth mixture.
6. Close the lid, select MEAT, and cook for 35 minutes.
7. When the cooking is complete, use a natural pressure release.
8. Serve immediately.

Lamb Shanks

Yield: 2 servings
Preparation Time: 15 minutes
Cooking Time: 40 minutes
Total Time: 55 minutes
Ingredients:
2 pounds lamb shanks, trimmed
Salt and pepper to taste
1 tablespoon olive oil
10 whole garlic cloves, peeled
1 cup chicken broth
1 tablespoon tomato paste
½ teaspoon dried rosemary, crushed
2 tablespoons fresh lemon juice
1 tablespoon unsalted butter

Directions:
1. Season shanks with salt and pepper.
2. Place the oil in the Instant Pot and select SAUTÉ. Add the shanks and sear for 3–4 minutes per side or until browned completely.
3. Add the garlic cloves and cook for about 1 minute.
4. Press CANCEL and stir in remaining ingredients.
5. Close the lid, select MANUAL, and cook at high pressure for 30 minutes.
6. When the cooking is complete, use a natural pressure release.

7. Remove the lid and with tongs, transfer the lamb shanks onto a platter.

8. Select SAUTÉ and cook for about 5 minutes to thicken the cooking liquid.

9. Stir in lemon juice and butter until smooth.

10. Press CANCEL and pour sauce over shanks.

11. Serve immediately.

Nutritional Information (Per Serving)
Calories: 1007
Fat: 47 g
Net Carbohydrates: 6.6 g
Protein: 31.3 g

Lamb Curry

Yield: 4 servings
Preparation Time: 15 minutes
Cooking Time: 35 minutes
Total Time: 50 minutes
Ingredients:
1 pound lamb shoulder, cut into bite sized pieces
1 tablespoon curry powder, divided
1 teaspoon red chili powder
¼ cup unsweetened coconut milk
2 tablespoons coconut cream
1 tablespoon coconut oil
1 medium yellow onion, chopped
½ cup chicken broth
1 tablespoon fresh lemon juice
Salt and pepper to taste
2 tablespoons fresh cilantro, chopped

Directions:
1. In a large bowl, add lamb, ½ tablespoon of curry powder, coconut milk, and coconut cream and stir to combine. Keep aside for at least 20 minutes.

2. Remove lamb from bowl, reserving the cream mixture.

3. Place the oil in the Instant Pot and select SAUTÉ. Add the onion and garlic and cook for 3–4 minutes.

4. Add remaining curry powder and chili powder and cook for about 1 minute.

5. Add lamb and cook for about 5 minutes.

6. Press CANCEL and stir in broth, lemon juice, salt, and pepper.

7. Close the lid, select MANUAL, and cook at high pressure for 20 minutes.

8. When the cooking is complete, do a quick pressure release.

9. Remove the lid and select SAUTÉ.

10. Stir in the reserved cream mixture and cook for 4–5 minutes, stirring occasionally.

11. Serve immediately with the garnishing of cilantro.

Nutritional Information (Per Serving)
Calories: 316
Fat: 16.6 g
Net Carbohydrates: 5.7 g
Protein: 33.5 g

CHAPTER SIX

Fish and Seafood

Salmon in Green Sauce

Yield: 4 servings
Preparation Time: 15 minutes
Cooking Time: 12 minutes
Total Time: 27 minutes
Ingredients:
1 avocado, peeled, pitted, and chopped
3 garlic cloves, chopped
½ cup fresh basil, chopped
1 tablespoon capers
1 tablespoon fresh lemon zest, grated finely
Salt and pepper to taste
4 (6-ounce) salmon fillets

Directions:
1. Grease a large piece of foil.
2. In a large bowl, add all ingredients except salmon and water and with a fork, mash completely.
3. Place fillets in the center of foil and top with the avocado mixture evenly.
4. Fold the foil around fillets to seal it.
5. In the bottom of Instant Pot, arrange a steamer trivet and pour 1 cup of water.
6. Place the foil packet on top of the trivet.
7. Close the lid, select MANUAL, and cook at high pressure for 8 minutes.
8. When the cooking is complete, use a natural pressure release.
9. Preheat the broiler of oven.

10. Open the lid and transfer the salmon fillets onto a broiler pan.

11. Broil for 3–4 minutes.

12. Serve warm.

Nutritional Information (Per Serving)
Calories: 333
Fat: 20.4 g
Net Carbohydrates: 2 g
Protein: 34.3 g

Lemony Salmon

Yield: 4 servings
Preparation Time: 15 minutes
Cooking Time: 7 minutes
Total Time: 22 minutes
Ingredients:
4 (4-ounce) salmon fillets
1 teaspoon garlic, minced
1 teaspoon fresh lemon zest, grated finely
1 cup chicken broth
1 tablespoon butter, melted
2 tablespoons fresh lemon juice
Salt and pepper to taste

Directions:
1. In the Instant Pot, add all ingredients and mix.
2. Close the lid, select MANUAL, and cook at high pressure for 7 minutes.
3. When the cooking is complete, use a natural pressure release.
4. Serve the salmon fillets with the topping of cooking sauce.

Nutritional Information (Per Serving)
Calories: 188
Fat: 10.3 g
Net Carbohydrates: 0.6 g
Protein: 23.4 g

Buttered Salmon

Yield: 4 servings
Preparation Time: 15 minutes
Cooking Time: 3 minutes
Total Time: 18 minutes
Ingredients:
¼ cup butter, melted
2 tablespoons fresh lemon juice
1 garlic clove, minced
2 tablespoons feta cheese, crumbled
¼ teaspoon dried oregano
Salt and pepper to taste
1 pound salmon fillets
2 fresh rosemary sprigs
2 lemon slices

Directions:
1. In a large bowl, add butter, lemon juice, garlic, feta, oregano, salt, and pepper and beat until well combined.

2. In the bottom of Instant Pot, arrange a steamer trivet and pour 1½ cups of water.

3. Place the salmon fillets on top of the trivet in a single layer and top with dressing. Arrange 1 rosemary sprig and 1 lemon slice over each fillet.

4. Close the lid, select STEAM, and cook for 3 minutes.

5. When the cooking is complete, do a quick pressure release.

6. Serve hot.

Nutritional Information (Per Serving)
Calories: 271
Fat: 19.7 g
Net Carbohydrates: 0.9 g
Protein: 23 g

Sockeye Salmon

Yield: 4 servings
Preparation Time: 15 minutes
Cooking Time: 7 minutes
Total Time: 22 minutes
Ingredients:
4 sockeye salmon fillets
1 teaspoon Dijon mustard
¼ teaspoon minced garlic
1 tablespoon lemon juice
¼ teaspoon onion powder
¼ teaspoon lemon pepper
½ teaspoon garlic powder
¼ teaspoon salt
2 tablespoons olive oil
1½ cups water

Directions:
1. In a bowl, combine the mustard, garlic, lemon juice, onion powder, lemon pepper, garlic powder, salt, and olive oil. Brush the spice mixture over the salmon fillets.

2. Pour the water into the Instant Pot. Lower the trivet.

3. Place the salmon fillets on the rack and close the lid.

4. Set the Instant Pot to MANUAL and cook at low pressure for 7 minutes.

5. When the cooking is complete, do a quick pressure release.

6. Serve and enjoy!

Nutritional Information (Per Serving)
Calories: 353
Fat: 25 g
Net Carbohydrates: 0.6 g
Protein: 40.6 g

Instant Salmon the Mediterranean Way

Yield: 4 servings
Preparation Time: 10 minutes
Cooking Time: 5 minutes
Total Time: 15 minutes
Ingredients:
4 salmon fillets
1 teaspoon Italian seasoning
1 rosemary sprig
1 cup water
2 tablespoons olive oil
¼ teaspoon garlic powder
¼ teaspoon lemon pepper
¼ teaspoon salt
15 asparagus spears
1 cup halved cherry tomatoes

Directions:
1. Pour the water into the Instant Pot and lower the trivet.
2. Season the salmon fillets with all of the spices, salt, and oil and arrange them on the trivet. Place the rosemary on top of the salmon.
3. Add the asparagus spears and top with the cherry tomatoes.
4. Close the lid, select MANUAL, and cook at low pressure for 5 minutes.
5. When the cooking is complete, do a quick pressure release.
6. Drizzled with olive oil and serve.

Nutritional Information (Per Serving)
Calories: 337
Fat: 18.5 g
Net Carbohydrates: 5.1 g

Protein: 37.5 g

Mahi-Mahi in Tomato Sauce

Yield: 6 servings
Preparation Time: 15 minutes
Cooking Time: 14 minutes
Total Time: 29 minutes
Ingredients:
3 tablespoons butter
1 (28-ounce) can diced tomatoes, no sugar added
1 yellow onion, sliced
2 tablespoons fresh lemon juice
1 teaspoon dried oregano
Salt and pepper to taste
6 (4-ounce) mahi-mahi fillets

Directions:
1. Place the butter in the Instant Pot and select SAUTÉ. Add all ingredients except fish fillets and cook for 8–10 minutes.

2. Press CANCEL and place fish fillets over sauce. With a spoon, place some sauce over fillets.

3. Close the lid, select MANUAL, and cook at high pressure for 4 minutes.

4. When the cooking is complete, do a quick pressure release.

5. Serve hot with the topping of sauce.

Nutritional Information (Per Serving)
Calories: 180
Fat: 6.9 g
Net Carbohydrates: 5 g
Protein: 22.5 g

Creamy Cod & Kale

Yield: 4 servings
Preparation Time: 15 minutes
Cooking Time: 22 minutes
Total Time: 37 minutes
Ingredients:
2 tablespoons coconut oil
1 small yellow onion, chopped finely
1 garlic clove, minced
1 large carrot, peeled and chopped
2 cups canned sugar-free chopped tomatoes with juice
2 tablespoons fresh parsley, chopped
2 cups water
1 pound frozen cod fillets
Salt and pepper to taste
2½ cups fresh kale, trimmed and chopped
½ cup heavy cream

Directions:
1. Place the coconut oil in the Instant Pot and select SAUTÉ. Add the onion and garlic and cook for about 3 minutes.
2. Add carrots, tomatoes, parsley, and water and cook for 3–4 minutes.
3. Press CANCEL and arrange a steamer basket on top.
4. Place cod fillets into steamer basket and sprinkle with salt and pepper.
5. Close the lid, select MANUAL, and cook at high pressure for 6 minutes.
6. When the cooking is complete, do a quick pressure release.
7. Remove the lid and transfer the fish fillets onto a platter.
8. With an immersion blender, puree the carrot mixture.
9. Select SAUTÉ and stir in kale and cream and cook for about 5 minutes.

10. Stir in fish fillets and cook for 3–4 minutes.

Nutritional Information (Per Serving)
Calories: 283
Fat: 13.6 g
Net Carbohydrates: 8.4 g
Protein: 28.7 g

Buttered Lobster

Yield: 2 servings
Preparation Time: 15 minutes
Cooking Time: 3 minutes
Total Time: 18 minutes
Ingredients:
2 pounds lobster tails, cut in half
2 tablespoons butter, melted
Salt and pepper
1 tablespoon fresh chives, minced

Directions:
1. In the bottom of Instant Pot, arrange a steamer trivet and pour 1 cup of water.
2. Place the lobster tails on the trivet.
3. Close the lid, select MANUAL, and cook at low pressure for 3 minutes.
4. When the cooking is complete, do a quick pressure release.
5. Transfer the lobster tails to a serving plate.
6. Drizzle with butter and sprinkle with salt, pepper, and chives before serving.

Nutritional Information (Per Serving)
Calories: 457
Fat: 9.5 g

Net Carbohydrates: 0.1 g
Protein: 86.4 g

Coconut Fish Curry

Yield: 4 servings
Preparation Time: 15 minutes
Cooking Time: 13 minutes
Total Time: 28 minutes
Ingredients:
1 pound white fish fillet, cut into small pieces
2 chilies, cut into strips
2 cloves garlic, chopped
1 tablespoon olive oil
6 curry leaves
1 tablespoon ground cumin
1 teaspoon chili powder
2 cups coconut milk
Salt and lemon juice for taste
1 cup cherry tomatoes
2 onions, cut into strips
1 tablespoon grated ginger
1 tablespoon ground coriander
½ teaspoon turmeric, ground
1 teaspoon chili powder

Directions:
1. Set the Instant Pot to SAUTÉ. Add the oil and curry leaves. Fry the leaves until they're golden, usually a minute.

2. Add in the ginger, onion, and garlic and sauté until they're soft.

3. Put the rest spices in there and sauté for a minute.

4. Deglaze with the coconut milk and then add in the fish, green chilies, and tomatoes.

5. Close the lid, select MANUAL, and cook at low pressure for 7 minutes.

6. When the cooking is complete, do a quick pressure release.

7. Season to taste before serving.

Nutritional Information (Per Serving)
Calories: 550
Fat: 41.4 g
Net Carbohydrates: 11.3 g
Protein: 32.1 g

Shrimp Zoodles

Yield: 4 servings
Preparation Time: 15 minutes
Cooking Time: 8 minutes
Total Time: 23 minutes
Ingredients:
4 cups zoodles (spiralized zucchini)
1 tablespoon chopped basil
2 tablespoons ghee
1 pound shrimp, peeled and deveined
1 cup vegetable stock
2 garlic cloves, minced
2 tablespoons olive oil
Juice of ½ lemon
½ teaspoon paprika

Directions:
1. Set your Instant Pot to SAUTÉ and melt the ghee with the olive oil in it.
2. Add the garlic and cook for one minute.
3. Add the lemon juice and shrimp and cook for another minute.
4. Stir in the remaining ingredients.
5. Close the lid, select MANUAL, and cook at low pressure for 5 minutes.
6. When the cooking is complete, do a quick pressure release.

Nutritional Information (Per Serving)
Calories: 277
Fat: 15.6 g
Net Carbohydrates: 5.9 g
Protein: 27.5 g

Shrimp Tomato Casserole

Yield: 4 servings
Preparation Time: 15 minutes
Cooking Time: 15 minutes
Total Time: 30 minutes
Ingredients:
1 Jalapeno, diced
1½ pounds shrimp, peeled and deveined
¼ cup chopped cilantro
1½ pounds tomatoes, chopped
2 tablespoons lime juice
2 tablespoons olive oil
1½ cups shredded Cheddar cheese
½ cup vegetable broth
1 teaspoon minced garlic
1 onion, diced

Directions:
1. Set the Instant Pot to SAUTÉ and heat the oil in it. Cook the onions for 3 minutes. Add the garlic and sauté for an additional minute.

2. Add tomatoes, cilantro and broth, and stir to combine.

3. Close the lid, select MANUAL, and cook at high pressure for 7 minutes.

4. When the cooking is complete, use a natural pressure release.

5. Stir in the shrimp, close the lid again, and cook at low pressure for 3 more minutes.

6. Do a quick pressure release.

7. Stir in the cheddar and lime juice.

8. Serve and enjoy!

Nutritional Information (Per Serving)
Calories: 421

Fat: 23.7 g
Net Carbohydrates: 8.4 g
Protein: 35 g

Cherry Tomato Mackerel

Yield: 4 servings
Preparation Time: 15 minutes
Cooking Time: 7 minutes
Total Time: 22 minutes
Ingredients:
4 mackerel fillets
¼ teaspoon onion powder
¼ teaspoon lemon pepper
¼ teaspoon garlic powder
¼ teaspoon salt
2 cups cherry tomatoes
3 tablespoons butter, melted
1½ cups water

Directions:
1. Grease a baking dish that fits inside the Instant Pot, with some cooking spray.

2. Arrange the cherry tomatoes at the bottom of the dish. Top with the mackerel fillets and sprinkle with all of the spices. Drizzle the melted butter over.

3. Pour the water into the Instant Pot and lower the trivet.

4. Place the baking dish on the trivet.

5. Close the lid, select MANUAL, and cook at low pressure for 7 minutes.

6. When the cooking is complete, do a quick pressure release.

7. Serve and enjoy!

Lobster Pasta

Yield: 4 servings
Preparation Time: 15 minutes
Cooking Time: 10 minutes
Total Time: 25 minutes
Ingredients:
3 lobster tails
1 cup half & half
2 cups water
4 cups zoodles (spiralized zucchini)
1 tablespoon arrowroot
1 tablespoon melt butter
1 cup shredded Gruyere cheese
1 tablespoon Worcestershire sauce
½ tablespoon chopped tarragon

Directions:
1. Combine the water and lobster tails in your Instant Pot.
2. Close the lid, select MANUAL, and cook at low pressure for 5 minutes.
3. Do a quick pressure release and transfer the lobster to a plate. Let it cool until easy to handle. Spoon out the meat from the tails and place in a bowl.
4. Discard the cooking liquid from the pot and combine the Half & Half, arrowroot, butter, and Worcestershire sauce in it.
5. Set the Instant Pot to SAUTÉ and cook the sauce for 2 minutes.

6. Stir in the lobster, zoodles, and cheese.

7. Cook for 3 minutes.

8. Sprinkle with tarragon and serve.

Nutritional Information (Per Serving)
Calories: 276
Fat: 19.5 g
Net Carbohydrates: 5.2 g
Protein: 21.3 g

Lemon and Garlic Prawns

Yield: 4 servings
Preparation Time: 10 minutes
Cooking Time: 8 minutes
Total Time: 18 minutes
Ingredients:
2 tablespoons olive oil
1 pound prawns
2 tablespoons minced garlic
2/3 cup fish stock
1 tablespoon butter
2 tablespoons lemon juice
1 tablespoon lemon zest
Salt and pepper to taste

Directions:
1. Melt the butter with the oil in your Instant Pot on SAUTÉ.
2. Stir in the remaining ingredients.
3. Close the lid, select MANUAL, and cook at low pressure for 5 minutes.
4. Do a quick pressure release and serve.

Nutritional Information (Per Serving)
Calories: 236
Fat: 12.2 g
Net Carbohydrates: 3.4 g
Protein: 27.1 g

Hot Tilapia

Yield: 4 servings
Preparation Time: 15 minutes
Cooking Time: 35 minutes
Total Time: 50 minutes
Ingredients:
1 pound tilapia fillets
3 tablespoons fish sauce
2 tablespoons olive oil
1 red chili, minced
1 green onion, minced
3 teaspoons minced garlic
⅓ cup water
¾ cup coconut water
Salt and pepper to taste

Directions:
1. Whisk together the fish sauce, olive oil, and garlic with some salt and pepper. Coat the tilapia with this mixture.

2. Wrap the tilapia in a plastic wrap and place in the fridge for half an hour.

3. Add the water and coconut water to the Instant Pot. Lower the trivet.

4. Unwrap the tilapia fillets, and Place them on the rack.

5. Close the lid, select MANUAL, and cook at low pressure for 5 minutes.

6. When the cooking is complete, do a quick pressure release.

7. Serve topped with red chili, green onion, and the sauce.

Nutritional Information (Per Serving)
Calories: 175
Fat: 8.2 g
Net Carbohydrates: 3.3 g
Protein: 22.5 g

CHAPTER SEVEN

Vegetables

Creamy Mushrooms

Yield: 5 servings
Preparation Time: 15 minutes
Cooking Time: 4 minutes
Total Time: 19 minutes
Ingredients:
1½ pounds cremini mushrooms
4 garlic cloves, chopped finely
¼ teaspoon dried thyme
½ teaspoon dried oregano
½ teaspoon dried basil
2 bay leaves
1 cup vegetable broth
Salt and pepper to taste
¼ cup half-and-half
2 tablespoons unsalted butter
2 tablespoons fresh parsley leaves, chopped

Directions:
1. In the Instant Pot, add all ingredients except half-and-half, butter, and parsley and stir to combine.
2. Close the lid, select MANUAL, and cook at high pressure for 4 minutes.
3. When the cooking is complete, do a quick pressure release.
4. Open the lid and stir in half-and-half, butter, and parsley.
5. Serve warm.

Spinach with Cheese

Yield: 4 servings
Preparation Time: 15 minutes
Cooking Time: 10 minutes
Total Time: 25 minutes
Ingredients:
1 tablespoon butter
1 small yellow onion, chopped
4 garlic cloves, chopped
1 Serrano pepper, chopped
½ teaspoon ground cumin
¼ teaspoon ground coriander
1 tomato, chopped
10 ounces fresh spinach
Salt and pepper to taste
10 ounces cottage cheese, cubed
2 tablespoons cream

Directions:
1. Place the butter in the Instant Pot and select SAUTÉ. Add the onion, garlic, green chili, and spices and cook for 3–4 minutes.
2. Add the tomato and cook for about 2 minutes.
3. Press CANCEL and stir in spinach, salt, and pepper.
4. Close the lid, select MANUAL, and cook at high pressure for 2 minutes.
5. When the cooking is complete, use a natural pressure release.

6. Remove the lid and with an immerse blender, puree the spinach mixture.

7. Select SAUTÉ and stir in cottage cheese. Cook for about 2 minutes.

8. Press CANCEL and transfer spinach mixture onto serving plates.

9. Top with cream and serve.

Nutritional Information (Per Serving)
Calories: 125
Fat: 5 g
Net Carbohydrates: 5.7 g
Protein: 12.5 g

Broccoli in Cheese Sauce

Yield: 3 servings
Preparation Time: 15 minutes
Cooking Time: 10 minutes
Total Time: 25 minutes
Ingredients:
For Broccoli:
2 cups broccoli florets
1 tablespoon olive oil
¼ teaspoon. garlic powder
½ tablespoon smoked paprika
Salt and pepper to taste

For Cheese Sauce:
3 tablespoons unsalted butter
2 tablespoons almond flour
½ cups unsweetened almond milk
1 cup shredded Cheddar cheese
¼ teaspoon garlic powder

Directions:

1. For broccoli: in a bowl, add all ingredients and toss to coat well.

2. In the bottom of Instant Pot, arrange a steamer basket and pour 1 cup of water.

3. Place the broccoli into the steamer basket.

4. Close the lid, select MANUAL, and cook at high pressure for 2 minutes.

5. When the cooking is complete, do a quick pressure release.

6. Meanwhile, for cheese sauce: in a medium pan, melt butter over medium-high heat.

7. Add almond flour, beating continuously.

8. Slowly, add almond milk, beating continuously and cook for 2–3 minutes or until thickened.

9. Add cheese and garlic powder and stir until smooth.

10. Remove the lid of Instant Pot and transfer broccoli onto serving plates.

11. Top with cheese sauce and serve.

Nutritional Information (Per Serving)
Calories: 432
Fat: 38.9 g
Net Carbohydrates: 5.5 g
Protein: 15.6 g

Mixed Veggie Casserole

Yield: 8 servings
Preparation Time: 20 minutes
Cooking Time: 31 minutes
Total Time: 25 minutes
Ingredients:
1 tablespoon coconut oil
1 medium yellow onion, finely chopped
4 garlic cloves, chopped finely
2 tablespoons curry powder
2½ cups cauliflower florets
2½ cups broccoli florets
3 tablespoons arrowroot starch
Salt and pepper to taste
2 cups water
1 (14-ounce) can unsweetened coconut milk
2 cups fresh green beans, chopped

Directions:
1. Place the coconut oil in the Instant Pot and select SAUTÉ. Add the onions and cook for 4–5 minutes.

2. Add the garlic and curry powder and cook for about 1 minute.

3. Press CANCEL and stir in remaining ingredients except green beans.

4. Close the lid, select MANUAL, and cook at high pressure for 3 minutes.

5. When the cooking is complete, do a quick pressure release.

6. Remove the lid and select SAUTÉ.

7. Stir in green beans and cook for about 5 minutes.

8. Press CANCEL and serve immediately.

Nutritional Information (Per Serving)

Calories: 176
Fat: 13.9 g
Carbohydrates: 8.7 g
Protein: 3.5 g

Mushroom and Green Bean Casserole

Yield: 8 servings
Preparation Time: 20 minutes
Cooking Time: 12 minutes
Total Time: 32 minutes
Ingredients:
For Casserole:
2 tablespoons butter
1 small yellow onion, thinly sliced
Salt to taste
8 ounces fresh button mushrooms, sliced
1¼ pounds green beans, trimmed and halved
2 garlic cloves, finely chopped
1 teaspoon Dijon mustard
½ cup vegetable broth
5 tablespoons crème fraîche

For Crispy Onions:
1 medium yellow onion, sliced into thin rings
2 tablespoons tapioca flour
Salt to taste
Pinch of ground black pepper
3 tablespoons coconut oil

Directions:
1. For casserole: place the butter in the Instant Pot and select SAUTÉ. Add the onion and cook for about 5 minutes.

2. Add the mushrooms and salt and cook for about 5 minutes.

3. Press CANCEL and stir in the green beans, garlic, mustard, and broth.

4. Close the lid, select MANUAL, and cook at high pressure for 2 minutes.

5. When the cooking is complete, do a quick pressure release.

6. Open the lid and stir in the crème fraîche.

7. Meanwhile, for crispy onions: in a bowl, add onion rings, flour, salt, and black pepper and toss to coat well.

8. In a deep-frying pan, melt coconut oil over medium-high heat.

9. Add the onions rings and cook for 3–4 minutes per side.

10. Remove from heat and transfer onion rings onto a plate.

11. Transfer the cooked green bean casserole into a serving dish and top with the crispy onions.

12. Serve immediately.

Nutritional Information (Per Serving)
Calories: 122
Fat: 8.7 g
Carbohydrates: 7 g
Protein: 2.8 g

Creamy Cauliflower Rice

Yield: 4 servings
Preparation Time: 15 minutes
Cooking Time: 8 minutes
Total Time: 23 minutes
Ingredients:
2 cups cauliflower, grated into rice consistency
½ cup sharp Cheddar cheese, shredded
½ cup half-and-half
2 tablespoons cream cheese, softened
Salt and pepper to taste

Directions:
1. In a heatproof bowl that fits in your Instant Pot, add all ingredients and stir to combine.
2. Cover the bowl with a piece of foil.
3. In the bottom of Instant Pot, arrange a steamer trivet and pour 1½ cups of water.
4. Place the bowl on top of the trivet.
5. Close the lid, select MANUAL, and cook at low pressure for 5 minutes.
6. Meanwhile, preheat the broiler of oven.
7. When the cooking is complete, do a natural pressure release for 10 minutes. Quick release the remaining pressure.
8. Open the lid and transfer the bowl onto a counter.
9. Remove the foil and broil for 2–3 minutes.
10. Remove from oven and serve hot.

Nutritional Information (Per Serving)
Calories: 126
Fat: 10 g
Net Carbohydrates: 3 g
Protein: 5.8 g

Bok Choy with Sesame

Yield: 4 servings
Preparation Time: 10 minutes
Cooking Time: 4 minutes
Total Time: 14 minutes
Ingredients:
1 head bok choy
1 tablespoon sesame seeds
1 teaspoon soy sauce
2 tablespoons sesame oil
¼ teaspoon garlic powder
¼ teaspoon salt
1½ cups water

Directions:
1. Pour the water into the Instant Pot and lower a steamer basket.

2. Place the bok choy in the basket.

3. Close the lid, select MANUAL, and cook at high pressure for 4 minutes.

4. When the cooking is complete, do a quick pressure release.

5. Transfer the bok choy to a cutting board, chop it, and transfer to a bowl.

6. Add the rest of the ingredients. Toss to combine.

7. Serve and enjoy!

Nutritional Information (Per Serving)
Calories: 102
Fat: 8.3 g
Net Carbohydrates: 2.9 g
Protein: 3.7 g

Ketogenic Eggplants and Spinach

Yield: 4 servings
Preparation Time: 10 minutes
Cooking Time: 6 minutes
Total Time: 16 minutes
Ingredients:
2 tablespoons coconut oil
4 cups cubed eggplants
2 cups chopped spinach
1 teaspoon five spice powder
1 cup vegetable broth
½ cup coconut milk
1 teaspoon chili powder
1 teaspoon salt
½ teaspoon pepper

Directions:
1. Set the Instant Pot to SAUTÉ and melt the coconut oil in it.

2. Add the eggplant cubes and cook for about 2 minutes.

3. Stir in the spinach and the seasonings.

4. Add the vegetable broth and coconut milk and stir to combine.

5. Close the lid, select MANUAL, and cook at high pressure for 4 minutes.

6. When the cooking is complete, do a quick pressure release.

Nutritional Information (Per Serving)
Calories: 164
Fat: 14.6 g
Net Carbohydrates: 3.6 g
Protein: 3.2 g

Tomato with Tofu

Yield: 4 servings
Preparation Time: 10 minutes
Cooking Time: 4 minutes
Total Time: 14 minutes
Ingredients:

1 cup diced tomatoes

1 block firm tofu, cubed

½ cup vegetable broth

2 teaspoons Italian seasoning

2 tablespoons jarred banana pepper rings

1 tablespoon olive oil

Directions:

1. Place all of the ingredients in the Instant Pot. Stir to combine the mixture well.

2. Close the lid, select MANUAL, and cook at high pressure for 4 minutes.

3. When the cooking is complete, do a quick pressure release.

4. Serve and enjoy!

Nutritional Information (Per Serving)
Calories: 68
Fat: 5.4 g
Net Carbohydrates: 2.3 g
Protein: 2.9 g

Buttered Asparagus

Yield: 4 servings
Preparation Time: 10 minutes
Cooking Time: 8 minutes
Total Time: 18 minutes
Ingredients:
1 pound fresh asparagus, trimmed
3 garlic cloves, peeled
3 tablespoons butter, softened
3 tablespoons Parmesan cheese, grated

Directions:
1. In the center of a foil piece, place asparagus and garlic and top with butter.
2. Curve the edges of foil slightly to avoid the leakage of butter.
3. In the bottom of Instant Pot, arrange a steamer basket and pour 1 cup of water.
4. Place the asparagus into the steamer basket.
5. Close the lid, select STEAM, and cook for 8 minutes.
6. When the cooking is complete, do a quick pressure release.
7. Transfer asparagus onto serving plates.
8. Sprinkle with Parmesan and serve.

Nutritional Information (Per Serving)
Calories: 108
Fat: 9.1 g
Net Carbohydrates: 2.8 g
Protein: 3.2 g

Dijon and Lemon Artichokes

Yield: 4 servings
Preparation Time: 15 minutes

Cooking Time: 20 minutes

Total Time: 35 minutes

Ingredients:

1½ cups water

2 artichokes

Juice of 1 lemon

¼ teaspoon salt

¼ teaspoon pepper

2 tablespoons Dijon mustard

2 tablespoons olive oil

1 lemon wedge

Directions:

1. Wash the artichokes well and trim them. Rub them with the lemon wedge.

2. Pour the water into the Instant Pot and lower the steamer basket.

3. Place the artichokes in the basket.

4. Close the lid, select MANUAL, and cook at high pressure for 20 minutes.

5. When the cooking is complete, do a natural pressure release for 10 minutes. Quick release the remaining pressure.

6. In a small bowl, mix together the lemon juice, mustard, olive oil, salt, and pepper.

7. Serve artichokes with the sauce.

Nutritional Information (Per Serving)

Calories: 108

Fat: 7.5 g

Net Carbohydrates: 5.4 g

Protein: 3.1 g

Zesty Broccoli and Cauliflower Bowl

Yield: 4 servings
Preparation Time: 15 minutes
Cooking Time: 6 minutes
Total Time: 21 minutes
Ingredients:
1 cauliflower head, chopped
1 pound broccoli florets
1 tablespoon capers
Juice and zest of 1 grapefruit
¼ teaspoon pepper
4 tablespoons olive oil
½ teaspoon salt
1½ cups water

Directions:
1. Pour the water into the Instant Pot and lower the steamer basket.

2. Place the cauliflower and broccoli inside the steamer basket.

3. Close the lid, select STEAM, and cook for 6 minutes.

4. Meanwhile, place the juice, zest, salt, pepper, capers, and oil in a bowl. Whisk to combine.

5. Do a quick pressure release and transfer the veggies to a bowl.

6. Pour the dressing over. Enjoy!

Nutritional Information (Per Serving)
Calories: 195
Fat: 14.5 g
Net Carbohydrates: 11 g
Protein: 4.8 g

Cauliflower Patties

Yield: 6 servings
Preparation Time: 15 minutes
Cooking Time: 20 minutes
Total Time: 35 minutes
Ingredients:
1 cauliflower head, chopped
1 cup shredded Cheddar cheese
2 eggs
¼ cup grated Parmesan cheese
1 cup ground almonds
3 tablespoons olive oil
1 teaspoon Italian seasoning
½ teaspoon salt
¼ teaspoon pepper
¼ teaspoon garlic powder
3 cups water

Directions:
1. Pour half of the water into the Instant Pot.

2. Place the cauliflower in the steamer basket and lower it into the pot.

3. Close the lid, select MANUAL, and cook at high pressure for 5 minutes.

4. Do a quick pressure release and let the cauliflower cool until safe to handle.

5. Transfer the cauliflower to a food processor. Pulse until finely ground.

6. Transfer the ground cauliflower to a bowl along with the eggs, parmesan, almonds, Italian seasoning, salt, pepper, garlic powder, and ¾ of the cheddar. Mix with your hands until fully incorporated.

7. Make patties out of the mixture.

8. Discard the water from the pot and wipe it clean.

9. Set the Instant Pot to SAUTÉ. Heat half of the oil in the pot and add half of the patties. Cook until golden on all sides. Repeat with the other half. Press CANCEL.

10. Transfer the patties to a greased baking dish. Top with the remaining cheese.

11. Pour the remaining water into the pot and lower the dish.

12. Close the lid, select MANUAL, and cook at high pressure for 2 minutes.

13. When the cooking is complete, do a quick pressure release.

14. Serve and enjoy!

Nutritional Information (Per Serving)
Calories: 278
Fat: 23.9 g
Net Carbohydrates: 3.4 g
Protein: 12.3 g

Mashed Cauliflower

Yield: 4 servings
Preparation Time: 10 minutes
Cooking Time: 4 minutes
Total Time: 14 minutes
Ingredients:
1 head cauliflower Head
3 tablespoons melt butter
1 cup water
¼ teaspoon pepper
½ teaspoon salt

Directions:
1. Chop the cauliflower and place inside a steamer basket.
2. Pour the water into the Instant Pot and lower the basket.
3. Close the lid, select MANUAL, and cook at high pressure for 4 minutes.
4. When the cooking is complete, do a quick pressure release.
5. Mash the cauliflower with a potato masher or in a food processor, and stir in the remaining ingredients.
6. Serve and enjoy!

Nutritional Information (Per Serving)
Calories: 113
Fat: 5.9 g
Net Carbohydrates: 4.1 g
Protein: 3 g

CHAPTER EIGHT

Soups, Stews and Chilies

Chicken and Salsa Soup

Yield: 6 servings
Preparation Time: 15 minutes
Cooking Time: 17 minutes
Total Time: 32 minutes
Ingredients:
2 pounds boneless, skinless chicken breasts
1 (15-ounce) jar salsa
2 Serrano peppers, chopped
2 tablespoons ground cumin
1 tablespoon red chili powder
Freshly ground black pepper to taste
5 cups chicken broth
1 cup water
1 (8-ounce) block cream cheese, softened and chopped

Directions:
1. In the Instant Pot, add all ingredients except cream cheese and stir to combine.

2. Close the lid, select MANUAL, and cook at high pressure for 15 minutes.

3. When the cooking is complete, do a natural pressure release for 10 minutes. Quick release the remaining pressure.

4. Remove the lid and with a slotted spoon, transfer the chicken breasts into a bowl.

5. With 2 forks, shred chicken breasts and then return to the pot.

6. Select SAUTÉ and stir in cream cheese. Cook for 1–2 minutes, stirring continuously.

7. Press CANCEL and serve hot.

Nutritional Information (Per Serving)
Calories: 463
Fat: 25.2 g
Net Carbohydrates: 6.1 g
Protein: 49.9 g

Cheesy Beef Soup

Yield: 8 servings
Preparation Time: 15 minutes
Cooking Time: 20 minutes
Total Time: 35 minutes
Ingredients:
1 tablespoon olive oil
2 pounds ground beef
4 garlic cloves, minced
2 tablespoons red chili powder
2 teaspoons ground cumin
20 ounces canned diced tomatoes with chilis
4 cups beef broth
Salt and pepper to taste
8 ounces cream cheese, softened
½ cup heavy cream

Directions:
1. Place the oil in the Instant Pot and select SAUTÉ. Add the beef and cook for about 10 minutes or until browned completely.

2. Press CANCEL and stir in remaining ingredients except cream cheese and cream and stir to combine.

3. Close the lid, select SOUP, and cook for 10 minutes.

4. When the cooking is complete, use a natural pressure release.

5. Open the lid and stir in cream cheese and cream until smooth.

6. Serve hot.

Nutritional Information (Per Serving)
Calories: 381
Fat: 22.1 g
Net Carbohydrates: 3.9 g
Protein: 39.2 g

Salmon Soup

Yield: 8 servings
Preparation Time: 20 minutes
Cooking Time: 21 minutes
Total Time: 41 minutes
Ingredients:
2 pounds salmon fillets
2 tablespoons coconut oil
2 cups carrots, peeled and chopped
1 cup celery stalk, chopped
½ cup yellow onion, chopped
2 cups cauliflower, chopped
4 cups chicken broth
1½ cups half-and-half
Pepper to taste
¼ cup fresh parsley, chopped

Directions:
1. In the bottom of Instant Pot, arrange a steamer trivet and pour 1 cup of water.

2. Place the salmon fillets on top of the trivet in a single layer.

3. Close the lid, select MANUAL, and cook at high pressure for 7–8 minutes.

4. When the cooking is complete, do a quick pressure release.

5. Open the lid and transfer the salmon onto a plate. Cut the salmon into bite sized pieces.

6. Remove water and trivet from Instant Pot.

7. Place the coconut oil in the Instant Pot and select SAUTÉ. Add the carrot, celery, and onion and cook for about 5 minutes or until browned.

8. Press CANCEL and stir in the cauliflower and broth.

9. Close the lid, select MANUAL, and cook at high pressure for 3 minutes.

10. When the cooking is complete, use a natural pressure release.

11. Open the lid and stir in salmon pieces, half-and-half, and pepper until well combined.

12. Serve immediately with the garnishing of parsley.

Nutritional Information (Per Serving)
Calories: 269
Fat: 15.7 g
Net Carbohydrates: 6 g
Protein: 25.3 g

Broccoli Soup

Yield: 6 servings
Preparation Time: 15 minutes
Cooking Time: 25 minutes
Total Time: 40 minutes
Ingredients:
1 tablespoon butter
½ of small yellow onion, chopped finely
2 large carrots, peeled and grated
3 cups broccoli florets
4½ cups chicken broth
3 cups heavy cream
1 cup Cheddar cheese, shredded
1 tablespoon hot sauce

Directions:
1. Place the butter in the Instant Pot and select SAUTÉ. Add the onion and cook for 4–5 minutes.

2. Press CANCEL and stir in the carrots, broccoli, and broth.

3. Close the lid, select MANUAL, and cook at high pressure for 15 minutes.

4. When the cooking is complete, use a natural pressure release.

5. Remove the lid and select SAUTÉ. Stir in the cream and cook for about 5 minutes.

6. Press CANCEL and stir in cheese and hot sauce.

7. Serve hot.

Nutritional Information (Per Serving)
Calories: 340
Fat: 30.5 g
Net Carbohydrates: 6.8 g
Protein: 9.1 g

Instant Pot Goulash

Yield: 6 servings
Preparation Time: 15 minutes
Cooking Time: 20 minutes
Total Time: 35 minutes
Ingredients:
2 pounds ground beef
1 red bell pepper, seeded and cut into strips
1 tablespoon minced garlic
½ teaspoon cayenne pepper
2 cups diced tomatoes
2 tablespoons olive oil, divided
1 onion, cut into strips
2 teaspoons sweet paprika
4 cups beef stock
Sour cream to serve

Directions:
1. Set the Instant Pot to SAUTÉ, and heat 1 tablespoon olive oil. Add the beef, and cook until it's browned and broken up. Transfer the beef to a bowl.

2. Heat 1 tablespoon olive oil in the pot. Add the red pepper and onion, and cook for a few minutes.

3. Add the rest of the ingredients and the beef.

4. Close the lid, select SOUP, and cook for 15 minutes.

5. Release the pressure naturally.

6. Serve with sour cream.

Nutritional Information (Per Serving)
Calories: 372
Fat: 14.9 g
Net Carbohydrates: 6.5 g
Protein: 49.4 g

Pomodoro Soup with Basil

Yield: 4 servings
Preparation Time: 10 minutes
Cooking Time: 20 minutes
Total Time: 30 minutes
Ingredients:
2 tablespoons olive oil
½ onion, diced
2 tablespoons tomato paste
3 cups vegetable broth
28 ounces diced tomatoes
A handful of basil, chopped
1 teaspoon balsamic vinegar
½ cup shredded Cheddar cheese

Directions:
1. Set your Instant Pot on SAUTÉ and heat the oil in it. Add the onions and sauté for 3–4 minutes.

2. Stir in the tomato paste and cook for 30–60 seconds.

3. Pour the broth over and stir in the tomatoes.

4. Close the lid, select SOUP, and cook for 10 minutes.

5. When the cooking is complete, use a natural pressure release.

6. Stir in half of the basil and the balsamic vinegar. Blend the mixture with a hand blender, until smooth.

7. Top with the remaining basil and serve.

Nutritional Information (Per Serving)
Calories: 196
Fat: 13.2 g
Net Carbohydrates: 8.8 g
Protein: 9.4 g

Bolognese Soup

Yield: 4 servings
Preparation Time: 15 minutes
Cooking Time: 25 minutes
Total Time: 40 minutes
Ingredients:
1 pound ground beef
1 cup onion, chopped
½ teaspoon oregano
½ teaspoon thyme
¼ cup tomato puree
14 ounces canned diced tomatoes
2 teaspoons minced garlic
2 cups cauliflower, diced
3 cups chicken broth
½ teaspoon pepper
½ teaspoon salt
4 tablespoons olive oil
1 tablespoon chopped basil

Directions:
1. Set the Instant Pot to SAUTÉ and heat the olive oil in it. Add the onions and cook for about 3 minutes.

2. Stir in the garlic and cook for 1 more minute.

3. Add the beef and cook until browned.

4. Stir in the tomatoes and tomato puree. Cook for about 2 minutes.

5. Add the broth, salt, and pepper, and stir to combine.

6. Close the lid, select MANUAL, and cook at high pressure for 5 minutes.

7. When the cooking is complete, do a quick pressure release.

8. Open the lid and stir in the cauliflower.

9. Close the lid, select MANUAL, and cook at high pressure for 5 minutes.

10. Let the pressure drop naturally.

11. Serve topped with chopped basil.

Nutritional Information (Per Serving)
Calories: 411
Fat: 22.5 g
Net Carbohydrates: 8.5 g
Protein: 40.7 g

Mexican Chicken Soup

Yield: 8 servings
Preparation Time: 10 minutes
Cooking Time: 10 minutes
Total Time: 20 minutes
Ingredients:
2 cups chicken, cooked and shredded
4 tablespoons olive oil
½ cup cilantro, chopped
8 cups chicken broth
⅓ cup salsa
1 teaspoon onion powder
½ cup chopped scallions
4 ounces canned and chopped green chilies
½ teaspoon habanero, minced
1 cup celery root, chopped
1 teaspoon cumin
1 teaspoon garlic powder
Salt and pepper to taste

Directions:
1. Place everything in the Instant Pot. Give it a good stir to combine.
2. Close the lid, select SOUP, and cook for 10 minutes.
3. When cooking is complete, use a natural pressure release.
4. Serve and enjoy!

Nutritional Information (Per Serving)
Calories: 204
Fat: 14 g
Net Carbohydrates: 4.2 g
Protein: 14.4 g

Keto Chili

Yield: 4 servings
Preparation Time: 15 minutes
Cooking Time: 38 minutes
Total Time: 53 minutes
Ingredients:
2 tablespoons olive oil
½ teaspoon cumin
2 tablespoons tomato paste
2 pounds ground beef
1 cup tomatoes, diced
1 teaspoon chili powder
1 onion, diced
1 cup beef broth
1 teaspoon minced garlic
Salt and pepper to taste

Directions:
1. Set the Instant Pot to SAUTÉ and heat the olive oil in it.
2. Cook the onions for about 2 minutes. Add the garlic and cook for 1 more minute.
3. Add the beef and cook until it is browned, breaking it with a spatula.
4. Stir in the tomato paste and spices and cook for 1 more minute.
5. Stir in the broth and tomatoes.
6. Close the lid, select MEAT/STEW, and cook for 30 minutes.
7. When the cooking is complete, do a quick pressure release.

Nutritional Information (Per Serving)
Calories: 505
Fat: 33.5 g
Net Carbohydrates: 5.1 g
Protein: 42.7 g

Creamy Chicken Chili

Yield: 8 servings

Preparation Time: 15 minutes

Cooking Time: 20 minutes

Total Time: 35 minutes

Ingredients:

2 pounds frozen, boneless chicken breasts

1 (10-ounce) can sugar-free diced tomatoes with green chiles

2 jalapeño peppers, chopped

½ teaspoon ground cumin

½ teaspoon red chili powder

Salt and pepper to taste

4 cups chicken broth

8 ounces cream cheese, softened

¼ cup sour cream

Directions:

1. In the pot of Instant Pot, add all ingredients except cream cheese and sour cream and stir to combine.

2. Close the lid, select SOUP, and cook for 20 minutes.

3. When the cooking is complete, do a natural pressure release for 10 minutes. Quick release the remaining pressure.

4. Open the lid and stir in cream cheese.

5. Serve hot with the topping of sour cream.

Nutritional Information (Per Serving)

Calories: 358

Fat: 20.7 g

Net Carbohydrates: 2.7 g

Protein: 38 g

Turkey Chili

Yield: 8 servings
Preparation Time: 15 minutes
Cooking Time: 50 minutes
Total Time: 1 hour 5 minutes
Ingredients:
1 tablespoon olive oil
½ large yellow onion, chopped
8 garlic cloves, minced
2½ pounds lean ground turkey
1½ (15-ounce) cans sugar-free diced tomatoes with liquid
2 ounces sugar-free tomato paste
1 (4-ounce) can green chiles with liquid
2 tablespoons Worcestershire sauce
¼ cup red chili powder
2 tablespoons ground cumin
1 tablespoon dried oregano, crushed
Salt and pepper to taste
1 large avocado, peeled, pitted, and sliced

Directions:
1. Place the oil in the Instant Pot and select SAUTÉ. Add the onion and celery and cook for about 5 minutes.
2. Add garlic and cook for about 1 minute.
3. Add turkey and cook for 4–5 minutes.
4. Press CANCEL and stir in remaining ingredients except avocado.
5. Close the lid, select MEAT/STEW, and just use the default time of 35 minutes.
6. When the cooking is complete, use a natural pressure release.
7. Serve hot with the topping of avocado slices.

Nutritional Information (Per Serving)

Calories: 317
Fat: 17.9 g
Net Carbohydrates: 6.7 g
Protein: 30 g

Beef and Mushroom Chili

Yield: 8 servings
Preparation Time: 15 minutes
Cooking Time: 30 minutes
Total Time: 45 minutes
Ingredients:
1 tablespoon olive oil
2 pounds beef chuck roast, cubed
Salt and pepper to taste
2 tablespoons ground cumin
1 tablespoon chili powder
1 tablespoon paprika
8 ounces fresh baby Portobello mushrooms, chopped
1 large green bell pepper, seeded and chopped
1 teaspoon garlic, crushed
1 (15-ounce) can sugar-free crushed tomatoes
1 (6-ounce) can sugar-free tomato paste
1 cup beef broth
$\frac{1}{3}$ cup sour cream

Directions:
1. Place oil in the Instant Pot and select SAUTÉ. Add the beef, salt, and pepper and cook for 4-5 minutes.
2. Press CANCEL and stir in broth.
3. Close the lid, select MANUAL, and cook at high pressure for 15 minutes.
4. When the cooking is complete, do a quick pressure release.

5. Open the lid and stir in remaining ingredients.

6. Close the lid, select MANUAL, and cook at high pressure for 10 minutes.

7. When the cooking is complete, use a natural pressure release.

8. Serve hot.

Nutritional Information (Per Serving)
Calories: 310
Fat: 11.6 g
Carbohydrates: 8 g
Protein: 39 g

Pressure-Cooked Beef Stew

Yield: 4 servings

Preparation Time: 15 minutes

Cooking Time: 28 minutes

Total Time: 43 minutes

Ingredients:

3 tablespoons olive oil

1 pound beef, cubed

3 cups beef broth

½ onion, diced

28 ounces canned diced tomatoes

2 teaspoons minced garlic

1 carrot, sliced *optional*

1 red bell pepper, chopped

2 tablespoons parsley, chopped

1 teaspoon thyme

1 bay leaf

Directions:

1. Set your Instant Pot to SAUTÉ and heat the olive oil in it.

2. Add onions and cook for 3 minutes, or until softened.

3. Add the garlic and thyme and cook until they become fragrant, about 1 minute.

4. Add the beef and cook it until browned on all sides.

5. Dump the rest of the ingredients into the Instant Pot and stir to combine.

6. Close the lid, select MANUAL, and cook at high pressure for 20 minutes.

7. When cooking is complete, wait for 5 minutes before releasing the pressure quickly.

Nutritional Information (Per Serving)
Calories: 382
Fat: 25 g
Net Carbohydrates: 10.6 g
Protein: 26.3 g

Fish Stew

Yield: 6 servings
Preparation Time: 15 minutes
Cooking Time: 10 minutes
Total Time: 25 minutes
Ingredients:
3 cups fish stock
1 onion, diced
1 cup chopped broccoli
2 celery stalks, chopped
1½ cups cauliflower, diced
1 carrot, sliced *optional*
1 pound white fish fillets, chopped
1 cup heavy cream
1 bay leaf
2 tablespoons butter
¼ teaspoon pepper

½ teaspoon salt

¼ teaspoon garlic powder

Directions:

1. Set your Instant Pot to SAUTÉ and melt the butter in it. Add onion and carrots (if using), and cook for 3 minutes.

2. Stir in the remaining ingredients.

3. Close the lid, select MANUAL, and cook at high pressure for 4 minutes.

4. When the cooking is complete, use a natural pressure release. Discard the bay leaf.

5. Serve and enjoy!

Nutritional Information (Per Serving)
Calories: 294
Fat: 18 g
Net Carbohydrates: 6.1 g
Protein: 24.2 g

CHAPTER NINE

Dessert

Vanilla Custard

Yield: 6 servings
Preparation Time: 15 minutes
Cooking Time: 10 minutes
Total Time: 25 minutes
Ingredients:
6 large eggs
4 cups unsweetened almond milk
½ cup Swerve
1 teaspoon vanilla extract
¼ teaspoon ground cinnamon

Directions:
1. In a bowl, crack the eggs and beat well.
2. Add remaining ingredients except cinnamon and beat until just combined.
3. Transfer the mixture into a heatproof bowl.
4. Cover the bowl with a piece of foil. With a fork, make tiny holes in the foil.
5. In the bottom of Instant Pot, arrange a steamer trivet and pour 1½ cups of water.
6. Place the bowl on top of the trivet.
7. Close the lid, select MANUAL, and cook at high pressure for 7 minutes.
8. When the cooking is complete, do a natural pressure release for 10 minutes. Quick release the remaining pressure.

9. Open the lid and transfer the bowl onto a counter to cool completely.

10. Refrigerate to chill.

11. Dust with cinnamon and serve.

Nutritional Information (Per Serving)
Calories: 101
Fat: 7.3 g
Net Carbohydrates: 1.4 g
Protein: 7 g

Chocolate Mousse

Yield: 6 servings
Preparation Time: 15 minutes
Cooking Time: 6 minutes
Total Time: 21 minutes
Ingredients:
4 egg yolks
½ cup Swerve
¼ cup cacao powder
¼ cup water
1 cup whipping cream
½ cup unsweetened almond milk
½ teaspoon vanilla extract
¼ teaspoon salt

Directions:
1. In a bowl, add the egg yolks and beat well. Keep aside.

2. In a pan, add the Swerve, cacao, and water and beat until well combined.

3. Add the cream and almond milk and beat until well combined.

4. Cook over medium heat until just heated, stirring continuously.

5. Remove from heat and stir in vanilla extract and salt. Keep aside to cool slightly.

6. Add about 1 tablespoon of warm chocolate mixture into the bowl of egg yolks and beat until well combined.

7. Slowly, add remaining chocolate mixture, beating continuously until well combined.

8. Transfer the mixture into 5 ramekins.

9. In the bottom of Instant Pot, arrange a steamer trivet and pour 1½ cups of water.

10. Place the ramekins on top of the trivet.

11. Close the lid, select MANUAL, and cook at high pressure for 6 minutes.

12. When the cooking is complete, do a quick pressure release.

13. Open the lid and transfer the ramekins onto a counter to cool completely.

14. Refrigerate to chill before serving.

Nutritional Information (Per Serving)
Calories: 129
Fat: 12.2 g
Net Carbohydrates: 2.4 g
Protein: 3.6 g

Pumpkin Pudding

Yield: 6 servings
Preparation Time: 15 minutes
Cooking Time: 20 minutes
Total Time: 35 minutes
Ingredients:
1 cup heavy whipping cream, divided
15 ounces pumpkin puree

¾ cup Swerve

2 eggs

1 teaspoon pumpkin pie spice

1 teaspoon vanilla extract

Directions:

1. In a bowl, add ½ cup of cream and remaining ingredients and beat until well combined.

2. Transfer the mixture into a greased 6x3-inch baking dish.

3. Cover the baking dish with a piece of foil.

4. In the bottom of Instant Pot, arrange a steamer trivet and pour 1½ cups of water.

5. Place the baking dish on top of the trivet.

6. Close the lid, select MANUAL, and cook at high pressure for 20 minutes.

7. When the cooking is complete, do a natural pressure release for 10 minutes. Quick release the remaining pressure.

8. Open the lid and transfer the baking dish onto a counter to cool completely.

9. Refrigerate to chill.

10. Top with remaining cream and serve.

Nutritional Information (Per Serving)
Calories: 118
Fat: 9.1 g
Net Carbohydrates: 4.8 g
Protein: 3.1 g

Lemon Cheesecake

Yield: 6 servings
Preparation Time: 15 minutes
Cooking Time: 30 minutes
Total Time: 45 minutes

Ingredients:

¼ cup plus 1 teaspoon Truvia

8 ounces cream cheese, softened

⅓ cup Ricotta cheese

1 teaspoon fresh lemon zest, grated

2 tablespoons fresh lemon juice

½ teaspoon lemon extract

2 eggs

2 tablespoons sour cream

Directions:

1. In a bowl, add ¼ cup of Truvia and remaining ingredients except eggs and sour cream and with a mixer, beat on high speed until smooth.

2. Add eggs and beat on low speed until well combined.

3. Transfer the mixture into a 6-inch greased spring-form pan.

4. Cover the pan with a piece of foil.

5. In the bottom of Instant Pot, arrange a steamer trivet and pour 2 cups of water.

6. Place the spring-form pan on top of the trivet.

7. Close the lid, select MANUAL, and cook at high pressure for 30 minutes.

8. When the cooking is complete, use a natural pressure release.

9. Open the lid and transfer the pan onto a wire rack. Keep aside to cool slightly.

10. Meanwhile, in a small bowl, add sour cream and remaining Truvia and beat until well combined.

11. Spread cream mixture on the warm cake evenly.

12. Refrigerate for about 6–8 hours.

13. Cut into desired sized slices and serve.

Nutritional Information (Per Serving)
Calories: 183
Fat: 16.6 g
Net Carbohydrates: 5.3 g

Protein: 6.5 g

Chocolate Cheesecake

Yield: 6 servings
Preparation Time: 20 minutes
Cooking Time: 20 minutes
Total Time: 40 minutes
Ingredients:
For Crust:
¼ cup coconut flour
¼ cup almond flour
2½ tablespoons cacao powder
1½ tablespoons Swerve
2 tablespoons butter, melted

For Filling:
16 ounces cream cheese, softened
⅓ cup cacao powder
½ teaspoon monk fruit powder
½ teaspoon stevia powder
1 large egg
2 large egg yolks
6 ounces unsweetened dark chocolate, melted
¾ cup heavy cream
¼ cup sour cream
1 teaspoon vanilla extract

Directions:

1. For crust: in a bowl, mix together flours, cacao powder, and Swerve.

2. Add butter and mix until well combined.

3. Place the mixture into a parchment paper lined 7-inch spring-form pan and with your fingers, press evenly.

4. For filling: in a food processor, add the cream cheese, cacao powder, monk fruit powder, and stevia and pulse until smooth.

5. Add egg and egg yolks and pulse until well combined.

6. Add remaining ingredients and pulse until well combined.

7. Place the filling mixture on top of crust evenly and with a rubber spatula, smooth the surface.

8. Cover the spring-form pan with foil loosely.

9. In the bottom of Instant Pot, arrange a steamer trivet and pour 1½ cups of water.

10. Fold a larger piece of foil in thirds to make a sling. Arrange the foil sling on top of the steamer trivet.

11. Place the spring-form pan over foil and fold tops of sling loosely over cheesecake.

12. Close the lid, select MANUAL, and cook at high pressure for 20 minutes.

13. When the cooking is complete, do a natural pressure release for 15 minutes. Quick release the remaining pressure.

14. Open the lid and transfer the pan onto a wire rack to cool completely.

15. Refrigerate for 6–8 hours.

16. Cut into desired sized slices and serve.

Nutritional Information (Per Serving)
Calories: 433
Fat: 42.3 g
Net Carbohydrates: 7 g
Protein: 10 g

Carrot Cake

Yield: 8 servings
Preparation Time: 15 minutes
Cooking Time: 40 minutes
Total Time: 55 minutes
Ingredients:
1 cup almond flour
2/3 cup Swerve
1 teaspoon baking powder
1½ teaspoons apple pie spice
1 cup carrots, peeled and shredded
½ cup walnuts, chopped
3 eggs
½ cup heavy whipping cream
¼ cup coconut oil

Directions:
1. In a large bowl, mix together flour, Swerve, baking powder, and pumpkin pie spice.

2. Add remaining ingredients and with a mixer, beat until fluffy.

3. Place the mixture into a greased 6-inch cake pan.

4. Cover the pan with a piece of foil.

5. In the bottom of Instant Pot, arrange a steamer trivet and pour 2 cups of water.

6. Place cake pan on top of the trivet.

7. Close the lid, select MANUAL, and cook at high pressure for 40 minutes.

8. When the cooking is complete, do a natural pressure release for 10 minutes. Quick release the remaining pressure.

9. Open the lid and transfer the pan onto a wire rack to cool for about 10 minutes.

10. Carefully invert cake onto wire rack to cool completely.

11. Cut into desired sized slices and serve.

Chocolate Cake

Yield: 6 servings
Preparation Time: 15 minutes
Cooking Time: 20 minutes
Total Time: 35 minutes
Ingredients:
3 eggs
1 cup almond flour
2/3 cup Swerve
⅓ cup heavy whipping cream
¼ cup coconut oil, softened
¼ cup cacao powder
¼ cup walnuts, chopped
1 teaspoon baking powder

Directions:
1. In a large bowl, add all ingredients and with a mixer, beat until fluffy.

2. Place the mixture into a greased Bundt pan that fits in your Instant Pot.

3. Cover the pan with a piece of foil.

4. In the bottom of Instant Pot, arrange a steamer trivet and pour 2 cups of water.

5. Place Bundt pan on top of the trivet.

6. Close the lid, select MANUAL, and cook at high pressure for 20 minutes.

7. When the cooking is complete, do a natural pressure release for 10 minutes. Quick release the remaining pressure.

8. Open the lid and transfer the pan onto a wire rack to cool for about 10 minutes.

9. Carefully invert cake onto wire rack to cool completely.

10. Cut into desired sized slices and serve.

Nutritional Information (Per Serving)
Calories: 201
Fat: 19.6 g
Net Carbohydrates: 2.3 g
Protein: 5.9 g

Strawberry Cake

Yield: 4 servings
Preparation Time: 15 minutes
Cooking Time: 25 minutes
Total Time: 40 minutes
Ingredients:
1 cup chopped strawberries
2 tablespoons heavy cream
5 egg yolks
10 drops liquid stevia
4 tablespoons coconut oil
¼ cup coconut flour
2 teaspoons lemon juice
½ teaspoon lemon zest
¼ teaspoon baking powder
1½ cups water

Directions:
1. Pour the water into your Instant Pot. Lower the trivet.

2. In a bowl, whisk together the yolks, stevia, juice, zest, heavy cream, and coconut oil.

3. In another bowl, combine the remaining wet ingredients.

4. Combine the two mixtures gently.

5. Grease a baking dish with cooking spray and pour half of the batter in it. Add the strawberries. Top with the remaining batter.

6. Place the baking dish on the trivet.

7. Close the lid, select MANUAL, and cook at high pressure for 20 minutes.

8. When the cooking is complete, do a quick pressure release.

Nutritional Information (Per Serving)
Calories: 283
Fat: 23.7 g
Net Carbohydrates: 7.2 g
Protein: 5.8 g

Instant Apple Tart

Yield: 8 servings
Preparation Time: 15 minutes
Cooking Time: 30 minutes
Total Time: 45 minutes
Ingredients:
Crust:
½ teaspoon liquid stevia
2 cups almond flour
6 tablespoons melt butter
¼ teaspoon lemon zest
1 teaspoon cinnamon

Filling:
¼ teaspoon lemon zest
½ teaspoon cinnamon
3 cups sliced apples
¼ teaspoon liquid stevia
¼ cup butter

Topping:
¼ teaspoon cinnamon

Directions:
1. In a bowl, place all of the ingredients for the crust. Mix with your hands until well combined.

2. Grease a baking dish with cooking spray and press the crust into its bottom firmly.

3. Pour about 1½ cups of water into the Instant Pot and lower the trivet.

4. Place the baking dish on the trivet.

5. Close the lid, select MANUAL, and cook at high pressure for 3 minutes.

6. Meanwhile, combine all of the filling ingredients and let sit for 2 minutes.

7. When the crust is done, do a quick pressure release. Open the lid and remove the dish carefully.

8. Arrange the apple slices over the crust.

9. Return the dish to the Instant Pot.

10. Close the lid, select MANUAL, and cook at high pressure for 3 minutes.

11. Do a quick pressure release.

12. Sprinkle cinnamon over the tart.

13. Serve and enjoy!

Nutritional Information (Per Serving)
Calories: 214
Fat: 17.9 g
Net Carbohydrates: 10.4 g
Protein: 1.9 g

Keto Plantain Bread

Yield: 12 servings
Preparation Time: 15 minutes
Cooking Time: 40 minutes
Total Time: 55 minutes
Ingredients:
⅓ cup chopped walnuts
2 plantains, mashed
1 teaspoon baking powder
2 eggs, beaten
2 cups almond flour
6 tablespoons butter, melted
1 tablespoon vanilla
½ teaspoon liquid stevia
1½ cups water

Directions:

1. Pour the water into the Instant Pot and lower the trivet.

2. Whisk together the vanilla, eggs, plantains, and butter in one bowl.

3. Combine the dry ingredients in another bowl.

4. Gently combine both mixtures.

5. Grease a loaf pan with cooking spray and pour the batter into it.

6. Place the pan on the trivet.

7. Close the lid, select MANUAL, and cook at high pressure for 35 minutes.

8. When the cooking is complete, do a quick pressure release.

Nutritional Information (Per Serving)
Calories: 151
Fat: 10.9 g
Net Carbohydrates: 9.9 g
Protein: 3.2 g

Spongy Cherry Cake

Yield: 8 servings
Preparation Time: 15 minutes
Cooking Time: 30 minutes
Total Time: 45 minutes
Ingredients:
2 tablespoons butter
1 cup milk
1 cup almond flour
6 eggs
⅓ cup swerve
½ teaspoon cherry extract
1 teaspoon vanilla extract

½ teaspoon xanthan gum
Pinch of salt
1½ cups pitted and halved cherries
½ cup heavy cream
1½ cups Water

Directions:

1. Pour the water into your Instant Pot and lower the steamer trivet.

2. Grease a baking dish with the butter.

3. Place all of the ingredients, except the cherries, in your food processor, and pulse until smooth.

4. Pour the batter into the greased dish. Top with the cherries (skin side down).

5. Place the baking dish on the trivet.

6. Close the lid, select MANUAL, and cook at high pressure for 30 minutes.

7. When the cooking is complete, do a natural pressure release for 10 minutes. Quick release the remaining pressure.

8. Serve and enjoy!

Nutritional Information (Per Serving)
Calories: 160
Fat: 11.7 g
Net Carbohydrates: 12.4 g
Protein: 6.5 g

Lemon and Hazelnut Muffins

Yield: 4 servings
Preparation Time: 15 minutes
Cooking Time: 15 minutes
Total Time: 30 minutes
Ingredients:

1 tablespoon lemon juice

1 tablespoon Swerve

1 teaspoon lemon zest

1 egg

2 tablespoons melted coconut oil

¼ cup coconut milk

1 cup coconut flour

Pinch of salt

Pinch of baking soda

3 tablespoons chopped hazelnuts

1½ cups Water

Directions:

1. Pour the water into the Instant Pot and lower the trivet.

2. Whisk together the wet ingredients in one bowl.

3. Gently whisk in the dry ingredients, making sure there are no lumps. Stir in the hazelnuts.

4. Divide the mixture between 4 silicone muffin cups.

5. Arrange the cups on the trivet and close the lid. Cook at high pressure for 15 minutes.

6. Release the pressure naturally for 10 minutes, then quick release the remaining pressure.

Nutritional Information (Per Serving)
Calories: 376
Fat: 19.8 g
Net Carbohydrates: 18.6 g
Protein: 10.3 g

Chocolate Muffins

Yield: 6 servings
Preparation Time: 15 minutes
Cooking Time: 17 minutes

Total Time: 32 minutes

Ingredients:

1 egg

½ cup pumpkin puree

4 tablespoons melted coconut oil

1 teaspoon apple cider vinegar

¼ cup sugar-free caramel syrup

¼ cup cocoa powder

1 cup flaxseed meal

1 teaspoon vanilla

1 tablespoon Swerve

1½ cups water

Directions:

1. Pour the water into the Instant Pot and lower the trivet.

2. Whisk all of the wet ingredients in one bowl and combine the dry ones in another.

3. Gently combine the two mixtures.

4. Divide the batter between 6 silicone muffin cups.

5. Arrange the muffin cups on the trivet.

6. Close the lid, select MANUAL, and cook at high pressure for 17 minutes.

7. Do a quick pressure release.

8. Serve and enjoy!

Nutritional Information (Per Serving)

Calories: 210

Fat: 16.5 g

Net Carbohydrates: 4.9 g

Protein: 5.3 g

Easy Walnut Cookies

Yield: 12 servings

Preparation Time: 15 minutes
Cooking Time: 16 minutes
Total Time: 31 minutes
Ingredients:
20 walnut halves
1 egg
2 tablespoons Swerve
2 tablespoons melt butter
2 cups ground walnuts
½ teaspoon baking soda
1½ cups water

Directions:
1. Pour the water into the Instant Pot and lower the steamer trivet.
2. Combine all of the ingredients except the walnut halves, in a large bowl.
3. Make 20 balls out of the mixture.
4. Line a baking dish with parchment paper and arrange half of the balls on it.
5. Top with walnut halves and press to flatten them out.
6. Place the dish on the trivet.
7. Close the lid, select MANUAL, and cook at high pressure for 8 minutes.
8. Do a quick pressure release.
9. Repeat with the other batch.
10. Serve and enjoy!

Nutritional Information (Per Serving)
Calories: 183
Fat: 17.6 g
Net Carbohydrates: 3.3 g
Protein: 6.8 g

Conclusion

The low carb diet has gained popularity as more people start to recognize its benefits for their fitness goals. I hope this book not only shows you how to cook easy and delicious low carb meals in an Instant Pot, but also inspires you to create your own recipes.

Finally, I want to thank you for reading my book. If you enjoyed the book, please take the time to share your thoughts and post a review on the book retailer's website. It would be greatly appreciated!

Best wishes,

Lindsey Page